more sewing

HOME

for the

Over 35 fun sewing projects to beautify your home

CREATIVE PUBLISHING international

CHANHASSEN, MINNESOTA
www.creativepub.com

Copyright © 2002
Creative Publishing international, Inc.
18705 Lake Drive East
Chanhassen, Minnesota 55317
1-800-328-3895
www.creativepub.com
All rights reserved
Printed in U.S.A.

President/CEO: Michael Eleftheriou
Vice President/Publisher: Linda Ball
Vice President/Retail Sales: Kevin Haas

MORE SEWING FOR THE HOME
Created by: The Editors of Creative Publishing
international, Inc.

Executive Editor: Elaine Perry
Senior Editor: Linda Neubauer
Project Managers: Linnéa Christensen, Kathi Holmes
Senior Art Director: Stephanie Michaud
Cover Designer: Megan Noller
Desktop Publishing Specialist: Laurie Kristensen
Editorial Intern: Andrew Karre
Project & Prop Stylist: Joanne Wawra
Sewing Staff: Karen Cermak, Arlene Dohrman, Kathy Davis
  Ellingson, Wendy Fedie, Phyllis Galbraith, Bridget Haugh
Technical Photo Stylists: Jennifer Bailey, Karen Cermak,
  Arlene Dohrman
Studio Services Manager: Marcia Chambers
Photo Services Coordinator: Carol Osterhus
Lead Photographer: Charles Nields
Photographers: Graham Brown, Rex Irmen, Tony Kubat,
  John Lauenstein, Mark Macemon, Mette Nielsen,
  Andrea Rugg
Director of Production Services: Kim Gerber
Shop Manager: Daniel Widerski
Contributors: Clotilde, Coats & Clark, Conso Products Co.,
  Dritz Corp., Dyno Merchandise Corp., EZ International,
  Gosling Tapes, June Tailor Inc., Kirsch, Olfa Product
  Corp., Pellon Corp., Seams Great Products Inc.,
  The Singer Co., Stacy Industries Inc., Swiss-Metrosene
  Inc., Waverly (Division of F. Schumacher & Co.)

ISBN 1-58923-075-2

Printed on American paper by:
R. R. Donnelley
10 9 8 7 6 5 4 3 2 1

Creative Publishing international, Inc. offers a variety of
how-to books. For information write:
  Creative Publishing international, Inc.
    Subscriber Books
  18705 Lake Drive East
  Chanhassen, MN 55317

more sewing

HME

for
the

Over 35 fun sewing projects to beautify your home

CONTENTS

Introduction 7

Getting Started 9

Sewing with a Plan 10

Creating an Atmosphere 12

Fabric Selection 14

Construction Basics 20

Decorative Accents 25

Window Treatments

Measuring Windows 32

Curtain & Drapery
  Hardware 34

Pinch-pleated
  Draperies 36

Tiebacks 42

Hourglass Curtains 46

Fabric Rosettes 51

Reverse Roll-up Shade 52

Bishop Sleeve Curtains 55

Tent-flap Curtains 56

Top Treatments 59

Pouf Valance 60

Double Pouf Valance 61

Austrian Valance 62

Tapered Valance 64

Swags & Jabots 66

Padded Cornices 71

Bed & Bath

Sewing for the Bedroom
  & Bath 76

Sewing with Sheets 77

Duvet Covers 78

Tuck-pleated Dust Skirt 82

Tuck-pleated Pillow Sham . .85

Duvet Cover from Sheets . . .86

Reverse Sham Bedcover 89

Futon Covers 91

Fabric Screen 94

Swagged Table Topper 97

Sink & Vanity Skirts 99

Embellished Towels 100

Shower Curtains 102

Cushions & Pillows

Boxed Cushions with
  Welting 108

Button-tufted Cushions 113

Tie-tab Pillows 116

Mock Box Pillows 120

Double-flange Pillows 123

Index 124

Introduction

More Sewing for the Home is a helpful planning and coordinating guide for the do-it-yourself home decorator. You can use the items in this book individually to enhance your existing decor, or coordinate fabrics and styles for numerous projects to develop a new decorating scheme throughout your home. You'll find tips and techniques used by professional designers to help you plan and organize your projects and decorate your home in your own unique style. The materials lists, cutting directions, and instructions given are complete; you do not need to purchase patterns. Colorful photographs show you how your project should look at each step of construction, ensuring your success.

Start with a Plan

The first section shows you the steps to take to set up a home decorating plan. Whether you are sewing a simple accent, redecorating an entire room, or starting fresh with a new home, you will want to keep this overall decorating scheme in mind. You are encouraged to keep a decorating notebook, collecting samples of fabrics, wallcoverings, and accessories that work well with your plan. Learn all about fabrics: how to mix prints and colors, how to select the appropriate fiber and finish for the project, and how to clean and care for the finished items. Discover sewing techniques and designer details that give your sewing projects quality and individuality.

Windows First

Windows are often a first consideration when decorating a room because of their visibility and size. The style and fabric you select can establish the room's mood and character. In the second section of the book you will find a variety of window treatment styles, including pinch-pleated draperies, hourglass curtains, reverse roll-up shades, and tent-flap curtains. Top treatments, such as cornice boards, swags, and various valances, give you many decorating options. Whether your taste is sleek contemporary, cozy country, or elegant traditional, there are window treatment styles that will work for you.

Personal Spaces

Perhaps the areas of your home where you can be the most creative and adventurous with your decorating are the personal areas: the bedrooms and bathrooms. Each room can be decorated to suit the individual preferences and personalities of the people who use it most. In a master suite, for example, you may sew a bedding ensemble with a duvet cover, pillow shams, and dust skirt that coordinates with a fabric screen. In the accompanying bathroom, sew a shower curtain and sink skirt to match, and embellish the towels with coordinating accents. For a cozy, inviting guest bedroom, sew a futon cover and a swagged table topper.

Around the House

In the last section of the book, you will find several cushion and pillow projects to round out your decorating plan and add a personal touch to your home. Pillows and cushions are found in almost every area of your home, from the living room to the sun porch. Never underestimate the decorating power of pillows. With small splashes of color and interesting textures, they can wake up a quiet color scheme and create a warm, friendly atmosphere.

Getting Started

Sewing with a Plan

You are the decorator when you sew for your home. The prospect can be as overwhelming as planning and coordinating the window treatments, pillows, and accessories for an entire new home, or it can be as simple as selecting a fabric for a kitchen curtain. Often, however, the single sewing project becomes only a beginning for a plan to refresh or update a whole area of the house.

Start by looking at your decorating needs and sewing projects room by room. A home generally looks larger and more pleasing when colors and patterns flow easily from one room to the next. Colors and patterns should relate, but they may branch off into different color schemes and moods. Devise a plan for your sewing project as a whole, but then work at it step by step. Any project will seem more manageable when broken into smaller pieces.

Where to Start

Most designers start planning the color scheme and direction for a home with the first rooms that are seen. The entry and the living room are usually these focal points. If the dining room is connected to the living room, look at the entry, living room, and dining room as one unit when considering colors and moods.

From the dining room you may move into the second area, the kitchen and family room, and sometimes the utility room and a related bathroom. A separate look or mood may coordinate these rooms, but the colors and fabrics you select should be compatible with the colors you have selected for the living and dining rooms. Separate areas that adjoin in a great room should be treated as one unit.

The third area, the master bedroom and bath, is another distinct area that has a special mood. Bedrooms are personal areas that are more apt to have fabrics and colors that reflect your personality, tastes, and interests. The remaining bedrooms and baths for children or guests may have other color and fabric directions. A guest bedroom may do double duty as a sewing room, home office, or den.

Record Keeping

An important part of the sewing plan is a notebook with pocket folders so you have a place to collect samples and swatches. Organize your notebook into the four general areas of the home. Leave plenty of pages between sections for all the information you will collect for each room. Clip pictures, and fill your notebook with ideas. Look for a mix in fabrics and colors, and interesting uses of texture and trimmings. The more ideas you collect for each room, the better.

Keep window measurements, room plans, pictures, and snapshots for each room in this notebook, along with phone numbers of important resources. Use a sturdy tote bag for carrying heavy, bulky samples.

Sources of Ideas

For inspiration, save magazine pictures of rooms that you like. Some classic styles remain stable year after year. It is often the detailing of trims, colors, and fabrics that can update home furnishings.

Many designers keep design magazines and trade publications that will also give you ideas. Furniture stores, model rooms, and catalogs have photos of window treatments, pillows, and accessories that you can sew. Most major cities have model homes and showcase houses that show the newest in decorating trends. Wallcovering books are also inspirational sources of decorating ideas; they show ideas for mixing fabric prints and using borders and stripes.

Creating an Atmosphere

List five words that you and your family would use to describe the results you wish to achieve from your decorating. These words will evoke different feelings about color, fabric patterns, and texture as well as furniture design and shape. For a family room or kitchen you may think of sunny, bright, clean, crisp, and cheery—or rich, warm, mellow, cozy, and traditional.

Elegant, comfortable, or traditional might be appropriate for the living-dining area. Strong, masculine, and rustic might be words for a library, den, or bath. Contemporary, clean, spacious, and

dramatic might be words for a bedroom. For someone else the mood for a bedroom might be romantic, soft, plush, feminine, and comfortable.

In the photo above, the warm, creamy yellow background of the primary fabric is printed with cool, slightly muted blues and greens to create a calming, friendly atmosphere. A contrast of textures gives the scheme visual and tactile interest. Simply changing a color or fabric can change the feeling in the room and create a different overall effect. Use the chart on the opposite page to get you started with your own decorating ideas.

Guidelines for Decorating

Overall Effect	Suggested Colors	Fabrics & Textures	Items to Sew
Elegant, special, or refined	Refined colors: mauve, taupe, gold, metallic, ecru	Shiny fabrics or fabrics with sheen: silks, fine cottons, antique satins, moirés, rayon trims	Hourglass curtains (page 46), Austrian valances (page 62), swags & jabots (page 66), double flange pillows (page 123)
Comfortable, casual	Autumn colors: rust, tan, gold	Smooth to lightly textured finishes, no scratchy finishes: polished cottons, chintzes, warp sateens, casements	Tent-flap curtains (page 56), welted cushions (page 108), mock box pillows (page 120)
Cozy, restful	Soft to medium shades: blue, mauve, green	Softly padded or quilted fabrics, inviting prints: cotton sheetings, warp sateens, chintzes	Duvet covers (page 78), tuck-pleated shams & dust skirts (pages 82, 85), button-tufted cushions (page 113)
Practical	Multi-colors, medium shades: red, blue, orange	Washable or stain-resistant fabrics, overall prints: sheetings, cotton blends	Tapered valances (page 64), duvet covers from sheets (page 86), sink skirts (page 99), fabric screens (page 94)
Conservative, clean & neat, tidy, crisp	Light colors, warm tones: white, mauve, peach, ecru, maize	Fabrics with woven designs, nubby textures, allover prints: sheer linens, cottons, casements	Pinch-pleated draperies (page 36), hourglass curtains (page 46), padded cornices (page 71), reverse sham bedcovers (page 89)
Tailored, masculine	Earth tones, rich colors: rich rust & brown, intense blue & green	Geometrics, plaids, stripes: upholstery fabrics, tapestries	Reverse roll-up shades (page 52), tent-flap curtains (page 56), padded cornices (page 71), boxed cushions (page 108)
Cheerful	Bright, clear colors: pink, yellow, blue, green, orange	Bold florals & stripes, fabrics with contrasting colors: decorator cotton prints, warp sateens	Tent-flap curtains (page 56), reverse sham bedcovers (page 89), shower curtains (page 102), tie-tab pillows (page 116)
Romantic	Fresh colors: pastel pink, blue, green, peach, ivory	Fabrics that encourage touching: silks, polished cottons, sateens, florals, water-color prints, laces, eyelet borders	Rosettes (page 51), pouf valances (pages 60, 61), ruffled duvet covers (page 78), duvet covers from sheets (page 86), swagged table toppers (page 97), tieback shower curtains (page 102)
Contemporary	Neutral tones: beige, gray, ivory, cream	Textured or smooth fabrics: simple designs, solids, casements	Reverse roll-up shades (page 52), tent-flap curtains (page 56), padded cornices (page 71), welted duvet covers (page 78), welted cushions (page 108)
Traditional, classic	Reliable colors: green, white, blue, burgundy	Timeless fabrics: antique satins, jacquards, matelassés, linens, velvets	Pinch-pleated draperies (page 36), hourglass curtains (page 46), swags & jabots (page 66), boxed cushions (page 108)

Fabric Selection

It pays to use good quality fabrics for home decorating projects. A good quality decorator fabric usually lasts longer and results in a finer finished look. Some of the most popular home decorator fabrics are shown here and on the next pages to help you with your selection.

As a rule, the tighter the weave or higher the thread count (number of threads per inch), the stronger the fabric. Most decorator fabrics have a higher thread count than garment fabrics.

Many decorator fabrics have a stain-resistant finish. To test, drop a small amount of water on the sample. If the water beads up instead of soaking in, the fabric will repel stains. This is more of a concern for cushions, pillows, slipcovers, and upholstery than for window treatments. Also, make sure that the dyes do not rub off when the fabric is handled or rubbed between your fingers.

Consider the end use, and be sure that the fabric is appropriate to the function. A decorative top treatment for a curtain, for example, will receive little wear; if a simple style is selected, it can be changed easily to update a look. Fabric for such a project does not get the heavy use that a chair cushion does, nor is it used as long as the average drapery. Remember that the average drapery may hang in a room anywhere from eight to fifteen years.

When comparing costs for large amounts of fabric, consider that prints may cost more than solid fabrics because you will need more fabric to match the motifs. The larger the repeat, the more likely you are to waste fabric when matching.

Lightweight open weaves are often used for window treatments because they let in the sunlight yet offer more privacy than undraped windows. Casement fabrics **(1)** are loosely woven, with uneven yarns and open areas. The variation in the weave creates a design in the fabric. Polyester, cotton, or linen fibers may be used. Laces and eyelets **(2)** may look delicate and fragile but are easy to sew and provide a light, airy look. Wide borders and finished edges eliminate hemming. Sheers **(3)** vary in fiber content but are usually polyester for a sheer, transparent look. Imported sheers can be up to 118" (300 cm) wide with embroidered or decorative hems.

Fiber Content

Cotton is a basic, strong, all-purpose fiber for home furnishing fabric. It dyes well for vibrant colors and has good durability. It may be used as a blend with many other fibers.

Linen is strong, but it will wrinkle. If wrinkling is a concern, crush a handful of fabric tightly in your fist and release it to see if wrinkles are retained. Decorator fabrics usually do not have crease-resistant finishes.

Rayon and acetate are often used together or in blends for a rich, silky appearance. Acetate may stretch in draperies and may spot if it gets wet.

Polyester is used alone or combined with other fibers to add stability. With all synthetics, use a low iron temperature when pressing.

Decorator Fabric vs. Garment Fabric

Decorator fabrics can be more expensive than garment fabrics, but garment fabrics may not have all the features you need. Normally, garment fabrics are not treated with stain-resistant finishes, and they usually have a lower thread count so they are not as durable. Use garment fabrics if the item will get little or no wear and your goal is simply to create an effect. Some garment fabrics are not heavy enough for a drapery but may be acceptable as a curtain, valance, or dust ruffle.

If using garment fabric, preshrink it. If repeated washing will be necessary for an item, do not sew it with materials that cannot be washed, such as buckram or linings.

Mediumweight basics are versatile multipurpose fabrics used for window treatments, cushions, cornices, and fabric screens. Chintz (**1**) is a glazed, plain-weave cotton or cotton-blend fabric. This tightly woven fabric is available in solid colors or prints that are often large, traditional florals. Warp sateen (**2**) is a cotton or cotton blend that has a softer hand than chintz but feels heavier. Warp threads floating on the surface create a smooth, soft sheen. This fabric is multipurpose for draperies, bedspreads, cushions, and slipcovers. Antique satin (**3**) varies in fiber content and quality. It is a very drapable, mediumweight solid fabric, which has slubs and a sheen.

Sailcloth and duck are medium to heavyweight plain-weave fabrics in cotton or cotton blends. They have a matte finish, without the sheen of chintz or sateen, so they have a more casual appearance in either solids or prints.

Upholstery fabrics are generally durable and long lasting. Available in a variety of textures and fiber contents, they include nubby linens, napped nylon velvets, and smooth cottons.

Preview Fabrics at Home

When shopping for fabric, take along samples from the room, such as an arm cover from a sofa, pillows from a chair, carpet samples, wallcoverings, and paint chips. These samples will help you select what you will take home to preview. Colors are very difficult to remember without samples for matching.

When looking at fabrics in the store, set aside the ones that blend well with your samples and remove those that do not. Select several fabric samples to take home.

Because of the difference in lighting, fabric may not look the same in your home as it does in the store. Store lighting is usually all or part fluorescent, whereas home lighting is usually natural or incandescent. To see how a fabric looks in a home environment, look at it in daylight and under home artificial light.

When you get home, drape the sample close to or on the area where it will be used. Keep it there for at least 24 hours to see if you like it. If the colors do not work or you dislike the pattern, this trial period will help you select something on your second outing that is closer to the effect you want. If you have a lot of solid colors in your room and want to switch to a print, the room will become more active. Make sure that the fabric sample you take home is large enough to show the pattern and the effect it will have on the room.

If you are attempting to match a solid color, be aware that dye lots can vary from the sample. If a close match is necessary, be sure there is enough fabric on one bolt for the project or that other bolts have the same dye lot. When you order from a swatch, request a cutting of the current dye lot for approval before the goods are actually shipped.

Fabric Care

When selecting fabrics for home decorating, consider colorfastness, durability, and care required. Check the manufacturer's recommended cleaning method. This information may be printed on the selvage or on the end of the fabric bolt. The salesclerk should also be able to provide the care information for you.

When choosing drapery fabrics, keep in mind that you will need to be tolerant of small fluctuations in the length of draperies after you hang them. No fabric is completely stable; the looser the weave, the less stable the fabric. Looser weaves are also more affected by heat and moisture; in humid climates the hemline in a loosely woven drapery can rise and drop in length more than one made from a tightly woven fabric.

If the manufacturer recommends drycleaning, the fabric should not be washed. Washing can soften buckram headings and linings; it can also shrink the trimmings, linings, and decorator fabric differently.

Although draperies do not get as much wear as upholstery and carpeting, they are subject to sun fading and deterioration from dust, heat, and moisture. Water spotting on draperies is usually a problem for drycleaners to remove, so try to prevent rain stains.

It is recommended that draperies be cleaned after the pollen season for health reasons, especially if you or someone in the household has allergies. Draperies may need cleaning less frequently if dust is regularly removed and stains are immediately treated. The most effective way to protect draperies from dust is to be sure that windows are sealed tightly, because dust and pollen coming into your house from outdoors become trapped in your draperies. Changing or cleaning the filter on a forced-air furnace frequently will also protect fabrics in your home from dust.

To extend the life of your draperies, vacuum them periodically. Dust may also be removed by tumbling drapery panels for a few minutes in a clothes dryer without heat. Be sure to remove drapery pins before tumbling window treatments in the dryer. To prevent wrinkles, remove the drapery panels from the dryer as soon as it stops.

Also vacuum upholstered pieces regularly to prevent dust from accumulating on the fabric surface. Rotate cushions regularly to ensure even wear and to keep cushions from breaking down and becoming lumpy. Upholstery is always cleaned intact.

Many decorator fabrics are treated with a stain-resistant or water-resistant finish. If the item gets obviously soiled, it can be spot-cleaned in place with an appropriate stain remover for the fabric. The protective finish should be reapplied after laundering or drycleaning. A drycleaner can usually apply the finish for you.

No fabric will withstand strong exposure to the sun; however, a good-quality drapery lining will help protect draperies from sun fading. Keep lined draperies closed to prevent fading of carpet and upholstery. Even with care, colors will naturally fade over a period of time. If fading is a concern, sun films with ultraviolet filters can be applied directly to the window glass.

Mixing Patterns

There are six basic categories of patterns in fabrics, and any decorating plan may use several of them in the same room. All six patterns can be used effectively in one room if you have a balance of color along with pattern size and scale.

Solids are often used in flooring, carpeting, walls, wallcoverings, and window treatments.

Geometric prints, such as checks and plaids, are not strictly for sporty looks. Many soft, silk-like fabrics have treated finishes and can be used in living rooms for a casual, elegant look. As chair coverings and throw pillows, they blend well with other textures.

Medallion patterns are usually small in scale and are often used in wallcoverings and in fabrics for chairs and pillows.

Stripes in subtle colors are often used in casement draperies and foyer wallcoverings; bolder stripe patterns may be used on chairs and sofas.

Overall prints and florals are most easily used on larger pieces, such as sofas and chairs, or major areas, such as draperies and valances.

Combination prints use two or more of the above patterns, and look best when used on larger areas, such as sofas, draperies, and valances.

Tips from a Designer

Four to six different patterns tend to become eclectic.

Less pattern mix is often more contemporary in feeling.

Repeat one strong-patterned print at least once or twice in the room. For example, a strong print in a sofa could be repeated in a valance. If both areas are on the same side of a room, you could also cover a chair, bench, or cushion across the room.

Miniprints can be overdone. Do not repeat more than two miniprints in the same area, including wallcoverings. If you use two miniprints, their scale could be different and the colors reversed.

Compare the outfitting of a room with personal tastes in clothing. Several prints, colors, and textures can be worn together, but colors must be coordinated effectively, textures must feel right together, and there must be an accent or a point of interest.

Repeat strong accent colors more than once.

Have fun. Do not be afraid to let fabrics and colors reflect your personal taste. Take time to find out what your tastes and style preferences are. Then carefully follow the step-by-step process for decorating success.

Construction Basics

Cutting & Matching

Cut fabric on the true lengthwise and crosswise grain to *square* the ends. Squaring ensures that curtains will always hang straight. Some fabrics can be squared by pulling a yarn on the crosswise grain and cutting along the space.

Avoid prints that are obviously off-grain. If these fabrics are cut on-grain, the design motif will be crooked and impossible to match at seams and edges. Many prints and woven patterns are only slightly off-grain, but their unevenness may be more apparent once the curtains are hung. Square the

ends of these fabrics by cutting on a line of the design rather than on the crosswise grain.

Some decorator fabrics have a permanent finish which holds the threads in place. Chintz, polished cotton, and other permanent-finish fabrics can be squared by simply cutting straight across the ends.

To obtain the desired finished curtain width, you may need to seam several widths of fabric together. Match the design motif of the fabric carefully so that seams are as inconspicuous as possible.

Three Ways to Straighten Crosswise Ends

Pull one or two yarns across the width of the fabric, from selvage to selvage. Cut on the line that appears after yarns have been pulled out.

Use a carpenter's square to straighten fabrics that have a permanent finish. Place one side of square parallel to selvage. Mark along other side of square; cut on marked line. Or align selvage with corner of table; cut across end.

Locate a design that runs straight across the fabric on the crosswise grain. Cut along the design. Consider depth of hem or heading when determining placement of the design on the finished curtain.

How to Match Design Motifs

1) **Position** fabric widths right sides together, matching selvages. Fold back upper selvage until pattern matches; press foldline.

2) **Unfold** selvage, and pin the fabric widths together on foldline. Check the match from right side.

3) **Repin** the fabric so the pins are perpendicular to foldline; stitch on the foldline, using straight stitch. Trim off selvages evenly, leaving ½" (1.3 cm) seam allowances.

Railroading Wide Fabrics

To eliminate seams, *railroad* a fabric. To railroad a fabric, turn the fabric on its side so that the normal width of the fabric becomes the length. This technique can often be used on valances, cornices, and dust ruffles, but is particularly practical for short curtains and seamless sheer draperies when fabric is extra wide.

The advantage of making draperies without seams is that there is no unevenness or puckering where widths of fabric are joined. In sheer fabrics, having no seams has the additional advantage of eliminating shadows at the seams. Railroading may require less fabric, and it saves time because there are no seams to sew.

Seams & Hems

How to Sew a French Seam

All seams in home decorating sewing are ½" (1.3 cm) unless otherwise indicated. When cutting fabric, remember to add the seam allowances to the finished size of the item you are sewing. Use a seam appropriate to the fabric when none is specified.

Avoid placing a seam in the center of wide items such as bedcovers, top treatments, or round table toppers. Split the panels and put the seams on sides so you will have a wide, full panel in the center. On Austrian and pleated valances, hide the seams with a scallop or pleat.

Plain seams, stitched with right sides together and pressed to one side, are used if the item is to be lined. If the item is not lined, finish raw edges with a zigzag or multistitch zigzag. Or overlock the seam allowances together.

French seams are appropriate on sheer fabrics and unlined curtains, draperies, table toppers, and dust ruffles. Because all raw edges are enclosed, this seam is especially stable for washable items.

Serged seams are timesaving and practical for home decorating because the seam is stitched and overedged at the same time. The serger is a supplement to a conventional sewing machine.

Double bottom and side hems are standard for window treatments. The longer the panel and lighter weight the fabric, the deeper the hem should be. Use double 4" (10 cm) hems on curtains or draperies that are longer than window length. Be careful not to place a hem in front of the window; when light comes through the curtain, the hem or lining edges should not be visible. Double side hems are usually 1½" (3.8 cm).

1) Pin *wrong* sides of fabric together. Stitch a scant ¼" (6 mm) seam. Press seam allowance to one side. Trim any fraying edges.

2) Turn fabric panels so right sides are together to enclose trimmed seam allowance. Stitch ¼" (6 mm) from folded edge, enclosing first seam. Press to one side.

Serged Hems

Rolled edge sewn with 3-thread overlock stitch is durable and neat on lightweight fabrics. Use it on tablecloths, napkins, and ruffles that otherwise require narrow hem. Contrasting thread can be used for decorative detail.

Satin edge is sewn with short, narrow 3-thread or 2-thread overlock. This method is good on textured fabrics, because it is less bulky than rolled edge. Use textured nylon thread for better coverage.

Serged Seams

4-thread overlock seam is durable, nonstretch, self-finished seam. Use for long straight seams.

3-thread overlock seam is an alternative for 4-thread seam. Use with conventional straight stitches, if necessary, to reinforce and to prevent stretching.

2-thread overlock stitch is fast, neat technique for finishing plain seams or raw edges of fabrics that ravel. Edges may be overlocked either before or after seam is stitched.

How to Sew a Double-fold Hem

1) Turn under the full hem allowance; press. Turn cut edge under, aligning it to pressed foldline; press.

2) Straight-stitch on folded hem edge, using 8 to 10 stitches per inch (2.5 cm). When stitching several layers of bulky fabric, lighten pressure slightly and stitch slowly.

Alternative method. After pressing hem, fold back to right side, leaving a fold of fabric about ⅛" (3 mm) from hem edge. Set machine to blindstitch. Adjust zigzag stitch to take tiny bite.

1

2

3

4

5

6

7

8

9

10

Decorative Accents

Cords & Trims

The addition of a trim may be all that is needed to create a decorator look or embellish a special treatment. Fringe, tassels, braid, silk cord, lace, ribbons, and bows are custom trimmings that add fancy finishing touches throughout the home. Use them on window treatments, valances, and tiebacks as well as on pillows, cushions, and duvets.

Trimmings should be compatible with the mood of the room as well as the weight and care of the fabric. Silky braids and tassels are perfect partners with elegant high-gloss fabrics. Eyelet and lace edgings are essential to a romantic, feminine look. Be sure that washable trimmings are used on washable items.

To mark placement lines for trimmings, use a water-soluble marking pen or a marking pen with lines that evaporate. If pins distort the trim when it is temporarily positioned for stitching, use glue stick to hold the trim in place. If a project lacks interest after it is finished, an applied trim can save it.

Allow extra trim for mitering corners. To be sure that the miter is perfect, you may want to test the trim in place and then baste it in position before stitching, especially when a patterned braid or eyelet needs matching at the corners.

1) **Edgings** have one raw edge and one finished edge. Lace and eyelet edgings may be flat or preruffled and pregathered. The unfinished edge is stitched in a seam or under a hem. If used on the surface, the raw edge may be covered with a ribbon or braid.

2) **Twisted cords** are available with an attached woven banding that can be stitched in a seam allowance.

3) **Loop fringe** has continuous, uncut loops attached to a band heading. The heading may be stitched or glued onto a hem.

4) **Tasseled tiebacks** are decorative twisted cords with tassels for holding draperies or curtains open.

5) **Tasseled fringe** has small tufts or tassels attached to a heading. The heading may be stitched or glued onto a hem.

6) **Fringe** is made of loose strands knotted through a finished heading. The heading may be stitched or glued onto a hem.

7) **Ribbons** are available in a wide range of colors and widths for every decorative application. Grosgrain is a fine, narrow corded weave. Satin is a smooth weave with sheen. Velvet has dense pile weave on one side. Taffeta is crisp, shiny ribbon with plain, plaid, or moiré finish. Ribbons are stitched, glued, or fused onto the surface.

8) **Gimp** is a narrow decorative braid with a loop or scroll design in one or two colors, used to cover seams and raw edges. It may be glued or stitched in place.

9) **Braid** has several strands or cords braided together to form a flat surface trim. It is applied on the surface of an item, not in a seam, and is either stitched, glued, or fused in place.

10) **Band trims** have two finished edges. They are applied the same way as braid.

Trimming Ideas

Tie a wide ribbon and a narrow ribbon of contrasting colors in large bow for tieback or ties on chair seats.

Sew or fuse braid or banding along drapery edges. Use purchased trim, or cut stripes or strips from fabric.

Use flat braid down the sides or along the bottom edge of roller shades.

Use narrow ribbon as bows to tie quilts and comforters.

Sew twisted cording into the seams of knife-edge pillows.

Use straight and looped fringe as traditional trims on edges of Austrian valances.

Apply pregathered lace edging for quick hem on duvets, dust ruffles, and tablecloths.

Sew flat lace or eyelet on edges of pillow shams over solid colors.

Glue or sew gimp or banding on edges of lampshades.

Sew six tucks down center of duvet cover; press three each way. Sew a row of lace edging down outside edges of tucks. Repeat on pillow shams.

Four Ways to Gather Ruffles

Zigzag. Stitch ⅜" (1 cm) from raw edge over a strong, thin cord such as string, crochet cotton, or dental floss. Use wide zigzag setting so cord does not get caught in stitching. Pull up cord to gather.

Ruffler attachment. Make a test strip, and adjust ruffler to desired fullness. Measure test strip before and after stitching to determine length of fabric needed. Before ruffling lightweight fabrics, zigzag ⅜" (1 cm) from edge with widest zigzag to give ruffler teeth something to grasp.

Shirring foot. This foot is designed to lock fullness into every stitch, assuring evenly spaced shirring. Set stitch length for a long stitch; the longer the stitch, the greater the fullness.

Serger with differential feed. Adjust differential feed for gathering; use shirring foot, if desired. Serge near edge of fabric, trimming slightly. Serger gathers fabric automatically. Make a test strip and adjust differential feed to desired fullness. Measure the test strip before and after stitching to determine length of fabric needed.

How to Sew and Attach a Ruffle with a Heading

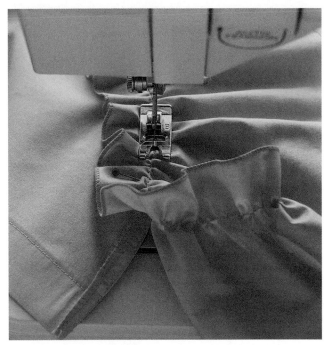

1) Hem both edges of strip to be ruffled with narrow double hem on conventional machine or rolled hem on a serger. Gather the ruffle strip the desired distance from upper edge, using any conventional machine gathering technique opposite.

2) Overlock edge, and press ½" (1.3 cm) to right side. Or turn and stitch double ¼" (6 mm) hem on right side of the edge where ruffle will be applied. Place wrong side of ruffle on right side of the fabric, with the gathering line on the hemline. Stitch ruffle in place. Allow extra fullness at corners.

How to Miter Corners on an Outside Edge

1) Place two lengths of trim, right sides together and edges even. Fold top trim at right angle to form diagonal at corner; press.

2) Slip-baste the two pieces together on the diagonal fold. Unfold trim.

3) Stitch on the line of slip basting on the wrong side. Trim the seams, and finish the edges.

Welting

Just as piping is used in garments to outline a fashion detail, welting is used in home decorator sewing to define and strengthen seams. Welting is fabric-covered cording, sewn into a seam to provide extra strength and a decorative finishing touch.

Fabric strips for welting may be cut on the bias or the straight grain. For more economical use of the fabric, they are cut on the straight grain. Bias welting is more flexible around corners and curves, however, and is preferable for small items like pillows.

Bias welting strips do not have to be cut on the true bias. Cutting the strips at an angle less than 45° gives the flexibility of bias grain but requires less yardage. For stripes and plaids, bias welting does not require matching.

To determine how wide to cut the fabric strips, wrap a piece of fabric or paper around the cording. Pin it together, encasing the cording. Cut both layers ½" (1.3 cm) from the pin. Measure the width, and cut strips to match.

Cording Sizes

5/32" (3.8 mm) is the usual cording for pillows, cushions, and slipcover seams. Cut fabric strip 1½" (3.8 cm) wide.

12/32" (1 cm) is slightly larger for similar applications. This size is appropriate for gathered welting. Cut fabric strip 2¼" (6 cm) wide.

16/32" (1.3 cm) is used for pillows and tablecloth edgings. It provides weight for a better hang at the bottom of bedspreads and comforters. Cut fabric strip 2¾" (7 cm) wide.

1" (2.5 cm) is jumbo cording that can be used for tiebacks and for decorative finishing. Cut the fabric strip 4½" (11.5 cm) wide.

How to Make and Attach Welting

1) Center cording on *wrong* side of strip. Fold strip over cording, aligning raw edges. Using zipper foot on right side of needle, machine-baste close to cording.

2) Attach welting on right side with raw edges aligned. Begin stitching 2" (5 cm) from end of welting; stitch on bastestitching line. To ease at rounded corners, clip seam allowances to bastestitching.

3) Stop stitching 2" (5 cm) from point where cording ends will meet. Leaving needle in fabric, cut off one end of cording so it overlaps the other end by 1" (2.5 cm).

4) Remove 1" (2.5 cm) of stitching from each end of welting. Trim cording ends so they just meet.

5) Fold under ½" (1.3 cm) of overlapping fabric. Lap it around the other end; finish stitching.

Window Treatments

Measuring Windows

After deciding on the window treatment, install the appropriate hardware, and then measure for curtains, draperies, shades, or top treatments. You will be determining the *finished length* and *width* of the treatment. The finished length is measured from the top of the heading or rod pocket to the bottom of the hem. The finished width is the width of the rod plus returns, and overlap for draperies. To determine the *cut length* and *width,* add the amounts needed for hems, rod pockets, seams, matching repeats, and fullness. Fill in a copy of the chart, right. Suggested hem allowances for the window treatments in this book are given in the Cutting Directions specific to the project. Use these measurements to estimate the amount of fabric needed. Pinch-pleated draperies require special measurement considerations for determining length and width and estimating fabric (page 37).

Use a folding ruler or metal tape for measuring; cloth tapes may stretch or sag. Measure and record the measurements for all windows separately, even if they appear to be the same size.

Special Measurement Considerations

Allow ½" (1.3 cm) clearance between the bottom of the drapery and the floor when measuring for floor-length draperies. This amount allows for cleaning and vacuuming, and provides sufficient clearance for electric cords. Also, if draperies sag or if floors are uneven, draperies will not drag on the floor.

Allow 1" (2.5 cm) clearance for loosely woven fabrics. This amount will provide an extra margin for them to stretch slightly without dragging on the floor.

Allow ½" (1.3 cm) clearance on sliding glass doors; more than this amount may let light gap at bottom.

Allow 4" to 6" (10 to 15 cm) drapery clearance above baseboard heaters for safety.

Allow 2½" (6.5 cm) clearance if carpeting is not installed. This amount provides approximately 2" (5 cm) for carpeting and padding, plus ½" (1.3 cm).

Underdraperies should be 1" (2.5 cm) shorter, ½" (1.3 cm) at top and bottom, so they do not show under the outer draperies.

Use the highest window in the room as the standard for measuring if windows are at different heights. Place all other draperies in the room at the same height from the floor.

Estimate Yardage

Cut Length	in. (cm)
For fabrics *not* requiring pattern match	
1) Finished length	
2) Double-fold bottom hem	+
3) Rod pocket/heading	+
4) Cut length for each width or part width	=
For fabrics requiring pattern match	
1) Cut length (figure as above)	
2) Size of pattern repeat (distance between motifs)	÷
3) Number of repeats needed*	=
4) Cut length for each width or part width: Multiply size of repeat by number of repeats needed	
Cut Width	
1) Finished width	
2) Fullness (how many times the finished width)	×
3) Width times fullness	=
4) Double-fold side hems	+
5) Total width needed	=
6) Width of fabric	
7) Number of fabric widths: Total width needed divided by width of fabric*	
Total Fabric Needed	
1) Cut length (as figured above)	
2) Number of fabric widths (as figured above)	×
3) Total fabric length	=
4) Number of yd. (m) needed: Total fabric length divided by 36" (100 cm)	yd. (m)
For wide sheers, which can be railroaded	
1) Finished width times 3 (fullness)	×
2) Number of yd. (m) needed: Total width needed divided by 36" (100 cm)	yd. (m)

*Round up to the nearest whole number.

NOTE: Add extra fabric for straightening ends.

NOTE: Half of the width will be used for each curtain panel. To piece panels, adjust width measurement to include 1" (2.5 cm) for each seam.

Determine Cut Length

Measure from the top of the rod to the desired length. To this length measurement, add the amount needed for lower hems, rod pockets, headings, and pattern repeat.

Lower hems. Add double the desired hem to finished length. For mediumweight fabrics, use a 4" (10 cm) double hem on floor-length curtains or draperies; add 8" (20.5 cm) to the length. For sheer and lightweight fabrics, a deeper double hem of 5" to 6" (12.5 to 15 cm) may be used. On short curtains or valances, use a 1" to 3" (2.5 to 7.5 cm) double hem.

Rod pockets and headings. For rod pockets with no heading, add an amount equal to the diameter of the rod plus ½" (1.3 cm) to turn under and ¼" to 1" (6 mm to 2.5 cm) ease. The amount of ease depends on the thickness of the fabric and the size of the rod. Lightweight fabrics require less ease; rod pockets for large rods require more. For rod pockets with headings, use the formula for a rod pocket, adding to it an amount twice the depth of the heading.

Pattern repeat. Prints must match across the width of the panels. Measure the distance between motifs, and add that amount to the cut length of each panel.

Determine Cut Width

To the finished width, add the amount needed for seams, side hems, and fullness.

Seams. For multi-width panels, add 1" (2.5 cm) for each seam. Panels that are not wider than the fabric do not require an extra amount for seams.

Side hems. Add 6" (15 cm) per panel for a 1½" (3.8 cm) double-fold hem on each side of panel.

Fullness. Fabric weight determines fullness. For laces and medium to heavyweight fabrics, use 2 to 2½ times the finished width of the curtain. For sheer and lightweight fabrics, use 2½ to 3 times the finished width.

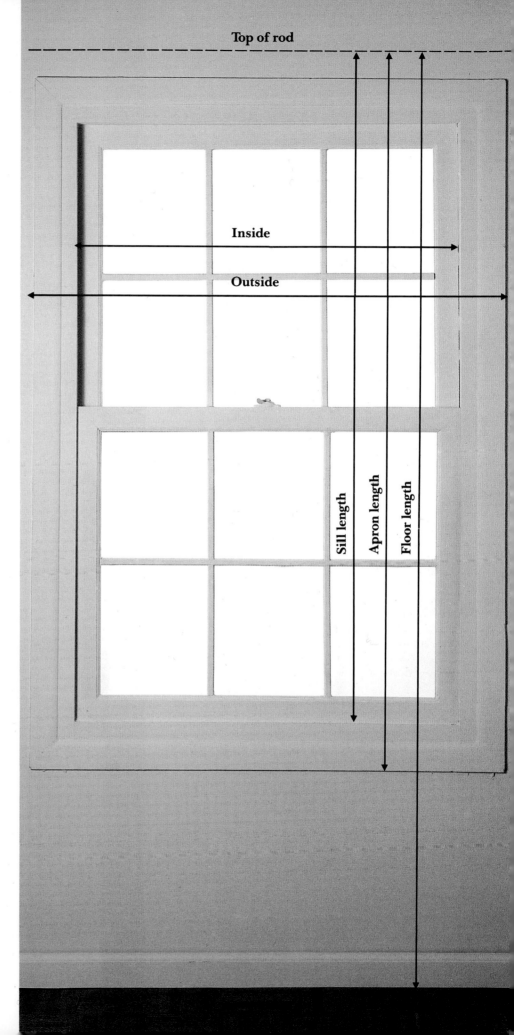

Curtain & Drapery Hardware

Whether your window treatment is stationary or traversing, the hardware you select can be decorative as well as functional. For ornate window treatments, traditional wood or metal poles with detailed finials are available, as well as decorative tieback holders. And sleek, contemporary hardware is available for a more understated look. Some treatment styles cover the rod entirely, calling for less expensive, nondecorative utility hardware.

Select and install the hardware you want before measuring for a window treatment. The cut length of fabric panels for curtains, draperies, and valances depends on the style and placement of the hardware.

Decorative Hardware

a) Metal rods and wood poles in various finishes and diameters are used with rings for hand-drawn traversing or stationary treatments when part or all of the rod or pole is always exposed. Without the rings, the rods and poles are suitable for swags or for stationary rod-pocket or tab styles. Stylish finials accompany the metal rods; wood poles may have finials or elbows. Unfinished wood poles can be painted, stained, or covered with fabric to fit perfectly into your decor.

b) Decorative traverse rods have a built-in mechanism of carriers and cording for opening and closing the treatment. Most often used for pleated draperies, the rods can have plain carriers or ring carriers. Tab carriers are also available, for hanging traversing tab curtains.

Utility Hardware

Narrow curtain rods are used for rod-pocket window treatments. They are available in various projections in single and double rod styles.

Wide curtain rods are available in 2½" (6.5 cm) and 4½" (11.5 cm) widths. They add depth and interest to rod-pocket window treatments. Corner connectors make these rods suitable for bay and corner windows, also.

Tension rods, used inside window frames for rod-pocket curtains and valances, are held in place by the pressure of a spring inside the rod. Because mounting brackets are not used, the woodwork is not damaged by screws.

Sash rods use shallow mounting brackets so the window treatment hangs close to the glass. Available flat or round, they are commonly used for stretched curtains on doors.

Conventional traverse rods, designed for pleated draperies, are available in white, ivory, and wood tones. Drapery hooks are inserted so the pleats conceal the rod when the treatment is closed. Valances or cornices are used over the top of the draperies to completely conceal the rod.

Flexible traverse rods are used for pleated draperies on bow windows.

Hardware Accessories

a) Concealed tieback holders fit behind the last fold of pleated or rod-pocket draperies to prevent the tieback from crushing the draperies. The projection is adjustable.

b) Cord-and-tassel tiebacks are used with concealed or decorative holders to hold draperies in place.

c) Holdbacks, as the name implies, are decorative accessories that hold back a stationary curtain or drapery without the use of tiebacks.

d) Swag holders, in a wide range of styles, support the draped fabric in swag window treatments. Some styles are meant to be concealed, while others are quite obviously decorative.

Pinch-pleated Draperies

Pinch-pleated draperies are a popular treatment for windows because draperies open to let in light and close for privacy. The pleats are spaced at intervals to control the fullness of the drapery. The more fabric that is pleated into the drapery panels, the fuller the draperies become.

Although pleater tapes are a quick solution for some draperies, the fullness, spacing, and depth of the pleats are limited when you use these tapes. The only way to have total control over the fullness and position of the pleats is the traditional buckram heading used in drapery workrooms.

Before you can determine the size of the drapery panels, you must determine the hardware and the mounting. For conventional rods, measure from ½" (1.3 cm) above the top of the rod to the desired finished length. For draperies that are mounted on decorative rods, measure from the pin holes in the rod to the desired finished length.

Remember to include stackback when mounting the rods. This is the amount needed at the side of the windows for the drapery to clear the window when

the drapery is open to its fullest. Actual stacking space will vary with the weight of the fabric, the fullness, and whether or not the drapery is lined, but it can be estimated at one-third the window width measurement. For center-pull draperies, allow for half the stacking space on each side of the window.

✂ Cutting Directions

Measure the window and follow the guidelines for curtains and draperies (pages 32 and 33). There are two basic measurements to consider: finished length and finished width. Estimate yardage and cut the lengths for drapery and lining, using the chart on the opposite page. These directions are for a pair of draperies.

YOU WILL NEED

Decorator fabric for draperies.

Lining fabric for lined draperies.

Conventional or decorative traverse rod.

Buckram, 4" (10 cm) wide, for heading.

Estimate Yardage

Drapery Length*	
1) Desired length as measured from rod	
2) 8" (20.5 cm) for heading	+
3) 8" (20.5 cm) for double hem	+
4) Cut drapery length	=
Drapery Width	
1) Rod width (from end bracket to end bracket on conventional rods; from end ring to end ring on decorative rods)	
2) Returns	+
3) Overlap [standard is 3½" (9 cm)]	+
4) Finished drapery width	=
Drapery Widths per Panel	
1) Finished width times 2, 2½, or 3 (fullness)	
2) Width of fabric	÷
3) Fabric widths needed: round up or down whole width	=
4) Divide widths by 2	÷
5) Number of widths per panel	=
Total Drapery Fabric Needed	
1) Cut drapery length (figured above)	
2) Fabric widths needed (figured above)	×
3) Total fabric length	=
4) Number of yd. (m) needed: total fabric length divided by 36" (100 cm)	yd. (m)

Lining Length	
1) Finished length of drapery (from top of heading to hem)	
2) 4" (10 cm) for double hems	+
3) Cut lining length	=
Lining Width	
1) Number of widths per panel (figure as for drapery widths per panel, above)	
2) Multiply widths by 2	×
3) Total fabric widths	=
Total Lining Fabric Needed	
1) Cut length (figured above)	
2) Fabric widths (figured above)	×
3) Total fabric length	=
4) Number of yd. (m) needed: total fabric length divided by 36" (100 cm)	yd. (m)

* For fabrics requiring pattern match, see page 32.

Drapery Pleats

Use the drapery pleat worksheet to determine the number and size of pleats and spaces per panel; this should be done after panels are sewn together and hemmed. The recommended amount of fabric required for each pleat is 4" to 6" (10 to 15 cm). The recommended space between pleats is 3½" to 4" (9 to 10 cm), approximately the same amount as the center overlap. If the worksheet calculation for the pleat size or the space between pleats is greater than the recommended amount, add one more pleat and space; if the calculation is smaller than the recommended amount, subtract one pleat and space.

Drapery Pleat Worksheet

Finished Panel Width	
1) Finished drapery width (figured left)	
2) divided by 2	÷
3) Finished panel width	=
Space between Pleats	
1) Number of widths per panel (figured left)	
2) Times number of pleats per width*	×
3) Number of pleats per panel	=
4) Number of spaces per panel (one less than pleats)	
5) Finished panel width (figured above)	
6) Overlap and returns (figured left)	−
7) Width to be pleated	=
8) Number of spaces per panel (figured above)	÷
9) Space between pleats	=
Pleat Allowance	
1) Flat width of hemmed panel	
2) Finished panel width (figured above)	−
3) Pleat allowance	=
Pleat Size	
1) Pleat allowance (figured above)	
2) Number of pleats in panel	÷
3) Pleat size	=

* Figure 5 pleats per width of 48" (122 cm) fabric, 6 pleats per width of 54" (137 cm) fabric. If you have a half width of fabric, figure 2 or 3 pleats in that half width. For example, for 48" (122 cm) fabric, 2½" widths per panel = 12 pleats.

How to Sew Unlined Pinch-pleated Draperies

1) Seam widths together as necessary. (Remove selvages to prevent puckering.) Use French or serged seams. Turn under and blindstitch or straight-stitch double 4" (10 cm) bottom hems.

2) Cut 4" (10 cm) wide buckram 6" (15 cm) shorter than width of panel. On wrong side of drapery panel, place buckram even with top edge and 3" (7.5 cm) from the sides.

3) Fold heading over twice, encasing buckram in fabric. Press; pin or hand-baste in place.

4) Turn under and blindstitch or straight-stitch double 1½" (3.8 cm) side hems. Determine size of pleat and space between pleats from worksheet (page 37).

Return   Pleat   Space   Pleat   Overlap

5) Mark the returns and overlaps on each panel; then mark the pleats and spaces. Mark a pleat just before the return and another next to overlap. Mark pleats next to any seams on side away from return. Pleat size can vary slightly within each fabric width. Keep spaces uniform.

6) Fold individual pleats by bringing two pleat lines together and pinning. Crease buckram on the fold.

7) Stitch on pleat line from top of heading to ½" (1.3 cm) below heading; backstitch to secure.

8) Divide into three even pleats. Crease the fold of the pleat with one hand while opening the pleat at the top of the heading.

9) Press fold straight down to meet the pleat stitching line. Two pleats form at the sides.

10) Pinch outer folds up to meet center fold. Finger press three pleats together, making sure they are all even.

11) Tack pleats with machine bar tack in center of pleat, ½" (1.3 cm) from bottom of buckram. Set machine for widest stitch, and stitch 4 to 5 times.

12) Insert drapery hooks. On a conventional traverse rod **(a),** top of hook is 1¾" (4.5 cm) from upper edge of drapery. On a ringless decorator traverse rod **(b),** hook is ¾" to 1" (2 to 2.5 cm) from upper edge. On a wood pole set **(c),** hook is ½" (1.3 cm) from upper edge.

How to Sew Lined Pleated Draperies

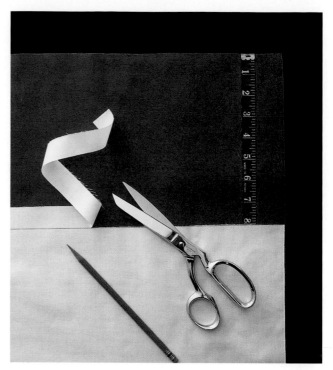

1) Stitch drapery fabric as on page 38, step 1. Repeat for lining, pressing under 2" (5 cm) double-fold hem. Place drapery panel on large flat surface. Lay lining panel on top of drapery panel, wrong sides together, with lower edge of lining 1" (2.5 cm) above lower edge of drapery panel; raw edges will be even at sides.

2) Mark lining panel 8" (20.5 cm) from upper edge of drapery panel. Trim on marked line.

3) Cut buckram the width of each drapery panel. Place buckram even with upper edge of drapery panel, on wrong side. Fold heading and buckram to wrong side; press.

4) Fold again, encasing the buckram in fabric, press. Lining edge will be even with the top of the heading. Pin or hand-baste in place.

5) Press under 1½" (3.8 cm) twice on sides, folding lining and drapery panels as one fabric. Tack drapery weights inside the side hems, about 3" (7.5 cm) from lower edge.

6) Stitch double-fold side hems, using blindstitch or straight stitch; stitch side hem in place at heading. Finish draperies as on pages 38 and 39, steps 5 to 12.

How to Dress Draperies

1) Draw draperies into the stacked position. Starting at the top, guide pleats into soft folds. If lined, catch lining in folds. Make sure depth of folds is even. Use grain of fabric as guide to keep pleats perpendicular to floor.

2) Staple a piece of paper or tie a piece of muslin around the pleats halfway between top and hem to hold them in place. Do not fasten so tightly that wrinkles appear.

3) Staple second piece of paper at the hemline. The draperies should hang straight from the rod. Leave tied for 5 to 7 days. Humidity will encourage the setting process.

Tiebacks

Jumbo welting tiebacks are a versatile
change from traditional straight or tapered
tiebacks. They can be braided, twisted,
knotted, or shirred to coordinate with
drapery and curtain panels. Welted tiebacks
with a shirred insert are perfect coordinates
with the soft, puffy look of bloused curtains
or lightweight tieback panels.

Placing a tieback low gives a visual effect of
widening the window; place it high to add
height. The most popular positions are
approximately one-third or two-thirds of the
window height, or at the sill. If cafe curtains
are used under the draperies or curtains, the
tiebacks are most often held back at the level
of the cafe rods.

To determine how long to make tiebacks,
measure around the curtain by holding a
tape measure loosely at the height you want
the tieback. Add 1" (2.5 cm) to the length for
seam allowances.

You can also estimate that for a pair of
draperies, a tieback is half the rod width, plus
4" (10 cm). It is generally not a good idea to
tie back a drapery that is wider than it is long.
If a drapery is tied back, it should remain
tied back as a stationary panel; wrinkles and
folds take several days to fall out.

How to Sew Braided Tiebacks

1) Cut cording 3 times the finished length of tieback; cut fabric strips 1½ times the length of tieback. Encase jumbo cording as in steps 1 to 3, below. Trim cording out of the ends; turn ends to inside, and slipstitch closed.

2) Overlap the three tubes slightly at one end. Hand-stitch tubes together, and braid. Cut other ends of tubes to desired tieback length; finish as for first end of tieback.

3) Use pin-on ring **(a)** or tack a curtain ring **(b)** in the center of each end. Attach rings to tieback holder on the wall.

How to Encase Cording

1) Cut cording 2 times the finished length needed. Cut fabric strip 2" (5 cm) longer than finished length, and width as on page 28. Fold strip around cording, *right* sides together, matching raw edges.

2) Use zipper foot to stitch loosely along cording, from one end of fabric to the other; do not crowd cording. Pivot, and stitch across the cording about ½" (1.3 cm) from edge of fabric.

3) Hold fabric loosely at stitched end; pull fabric from covered to uncovered end of cording, turning tube right side out to encase cording. Cut off stitched end of fabric and excess cording.

Jumbo Knotted Tieback

Cut cording 2 times the finished length of tieback plus 40" (102 cm) for knot. Cut fabric strips the length of tieback plus 20" (51 cm). Encase cording, page 43, steps 1 to 3. Tie big knot near center. Cut tieback to desired length. Trim cording out of ends. Turn ends to inside; slipstitch closed. Tack curtain ring on each end.

Jumbo Twist Tieback

Cut cording 2 times the finished length of tieback; cut fabric strips the length of tieback plus 1" (2.5 cm). Encase jumbo cording, page 43, steps 1 to 3. Trim cording out of ends. Turn ends to inside; slipstitch closed. Hand-stitch ends of tubes together, and twist. Tack curtain ring on each end.

Shirred Jumbo Welting Tieback

Cut cording 3 times the tieback length. Cut fabric strips 2 times the tieback length and 2" (5 cm) wider than circumference of cording. Fold strip around cording, *right* sides together. Encase cording, bottom of page 43, steps 2 and 3, gathering fabric as tube is turned. Finish ends, catching cording in stitching. Attach rings.

Shirred Insert Tieback

1) Cut insert 2 times finished length plus 2" (5 cm) and finished width plus 1" (2.5 cm). Cut lining 2" (5 cm) longer and 1" (2.5 cm) wider than finished tieback. Cut buckram ¼" (6 mm) narrower than finished size. Cut bias strips for welting (page 28) 2 times the finished length, plus 4" (10 cm) extra for finishing ends.

2) Gather both edges of the insert. Make welting (page 29). Machine-baste welting on right side of shirred strip in ⅜" (1 cm) seam. Pin right side of lining to right side of strip. Stitch ½" (1.3 cm) seam. Turn right side out.

3) Trim buckram to slight point at one end. Attach bodkin to pointed end, and insert buckram between gathered insert and lining.

4) Trim 1" (2.5 cm) of cording out of welting at ends. Turn under a double ½" (1.3 cm) hem at ends, and slipstitch in place. Attach rings in center of tieback.

Hourglass Curtains

Hourglass curtains take their name from their shape. They are held taut between sash rods at the top and bottom of the window glass, and then pulled in at the center to create the hourglass shape. Use tension rods, instead of sash rods, for mounting inside a window frame.

Because these curtains are held tight to the glass, they are a practical treatment for doors. They also work well on windows where there is not room for a return. They allow sunlight to get in and, for extra airiness, are attractive in lace and sheer fabrics.

You will need to take two length measurements: the length at the center of the curtain and the adjusted length at the sides. The adjusted length accommodates the pinching in of the fabric at the center of the window. Estimate 2" (5 cm) extra at the sides for every 12" (30.5 cm).

YOU WILL NEED

Ribbon or twill tape.

Sheer to lightweight decorator fabric.

Two sash rods, curtain rods with up to 1¼" (3.2 cm) projection, or spring-tension rods.

White heavyweight sew-in interfacing; ivory lightweight fusible interfacing, to prevent show-through, optional.

✂ Cutting Directions

Cut the fabric with the length equal to Measurement C plus four times the rod-pocket depth and four times the desired heading depth (page 32) plus 1" (2.5 cm) for turn-under. The cut width of the fabric is equal to two-and-one-half to three times Measurement A, depending on the desired fullness, plus 4" (10 cm) for 1" (2.5 cm) double-fold side hems. Seam fabric widths together, if necessary, using French seams (page 22).

Cut a strip of fabric for the tieback, with the length equal to two times Measurement B plus 1½" (3.8 cm). The cut width of the fabric strip is equal to twice the desired finished width of the tieback plus 1" (2.5 cm).

Cut one strip each of heavyweight sew-in interfacing and optional ivory lightweight fusible interfacing, with the length 1" (2.5 cm) shorter than the cut length of the tieback strip; the cut width is ⅛" (3 mm) narrower than the finished width of the tieback. Fuse the strips together.

1) Install rods. Tape a strip of ribbon or twill tape to door or window, outlining desired shape of curtain. Begin at lower outside corner of top rod, angling in desired distance to center, and then out to upper outside corner of bottom rod. Repeat for opposite side.

2) Measure width of curtain across top or bottom; this is referred to as Measurement A. Measure width of curtain across center; this is referred to as Measurement B. Subtract Measurement B from Measurement A; record the difference.

3) Measure the length of the ribbon down one angled side; this is referred to as Measurement C. Measure the length of the curtain down the center, measuring from the lower edge of the top rod to the upper edge of the bottom rod; this is referred to as Measurement D. Subtract Measurement D from Measurement C; record the difference.

How to Sew an Hourglass Curtain

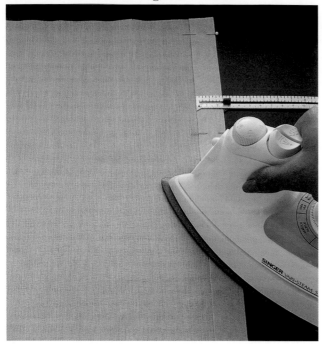

1) Seam fabric widths together, if necessary, using French seams (page 22). Press under 1" (2.5 cm) twice on sides of curtain panel; stitch to make double-fold hems, using straight stitch or blindstitch.

2) Press under ½" (1.3 cm) on upper edge. Then press under an amount equal to the rod-pocket depth plus the heading depth; pin.

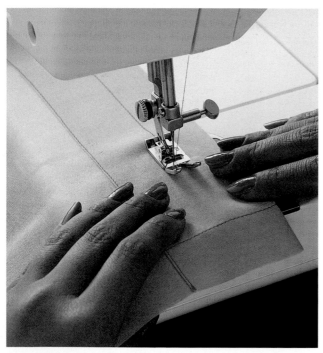

3) Stitch close to the first fold. Stitch again at the depth of the heading.

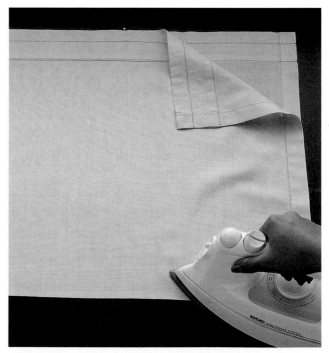

4) Repeat steps 2 and 3 for lower edge of curtain panel. Fold curtain in half crosswise, right sides together, matching top and bottom rod pockets and headings. Press foldline across center of curtain.

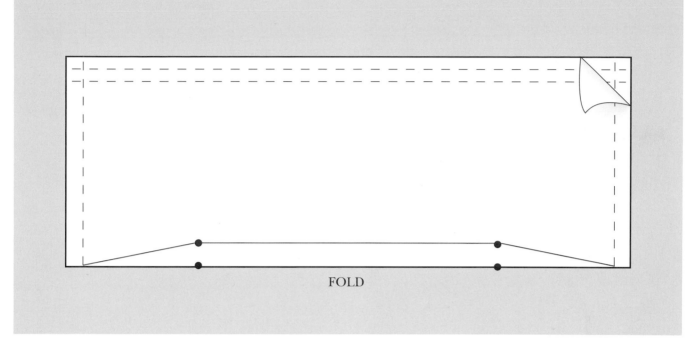

FOLD

5) Divide the difference between Measurement A and Measurement B in half. Then multiply this number by the amount of fullness allowed for the curtain. Measure this distance along pressed fold from one side toward center; pin-mark. Repeat for opposite side.

6) Divide the difference between Measurement C and Measurement D in half. Measure up from the fold at pin marks a distance equal to this measurement; mark. Draw a line between upper marks, parallel to the foldline.

7) Extend line to pressed fold at inner edges of side hems, using straightedge, if sash rods or spring-tension rods are used. If rods have up to a 1¼" (3.2 cm) projection, taper line to 4" (10 cm) from side hems. Stitch on marked line, making a long dart.

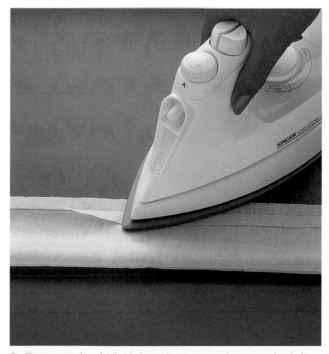

8) Press under ½" (1.3 cm) on one short end of the tieback. Fold the tieback in half lengthwise, right sides together; pin. Sew a ½" (1.3 cm) seam on long edge; press seam open.

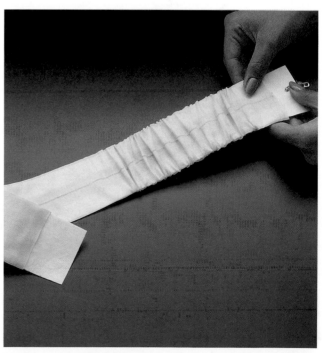

9) Turn tieback right side out, using safety pin or bodkin. Center the seam on back of tieback; press. Insert interfacing strip into tieback (optional ivory interfacing faces front).

(Continued on next page)

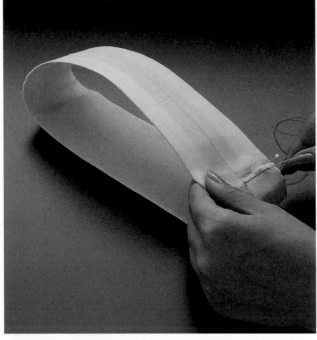

10) Insert unfinished end of tieback into pressed end, overlapping ½" (1.3 cm). Slipstitch ends together, making a circular tieback.

11) Place curtain through tieback. Insert the spring-tension rods or sash rods in top and bottom rod pockets. Mount curtain, check fit.

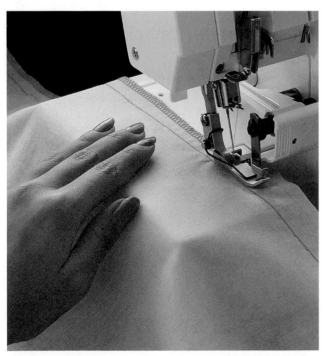

12) Adjust stitching of dart, if necessary. Trim fabric ½" (1.3 cm) from stitched dart; finish seam, and press.

13) Reinstall curtain. Secure tieback to center of curtain, using concealed safety pin.

Fabric Rosettes

Use fabric rosettes as decorative accents on hourglass curtain tiebacks or at the corners of swags, valances, and swagged table toppers. They need a fairly crisp fabric such as chintz or moiré to stand up; in a soft fabric they take on a draped look. Rosettes may be cut on either the crosswise grain or on the bias; they have a softer effect when cut on the bias.

The directions that follow are for a 7" (18 cm) rosette. For a smaller rosette, reduce cutting measurements proportionately. The finished rosette is as wide as the original cut strip.

✂ Cutting Directions

Cut fabric strip 7" (18 cm) wide and 72" (183 cm) long for 7" (18 cm) rosette.

How to Sew a Fabric Rosette

1) **Fold** strip in half lengthwise, wrong sides together; gather raw edges; stitch across short ends to round the corners. Trim excess fabric at ends.

2) **Roll** one of the rounded ends tightly toward center to make center of rosette.

3) **Continue** rolling loosely toward opposite end, tacking gathers together with needle and thread.

4) **Shape** "petals" with your hands. Hand-tack rosette in place.

Reverse Roll-up Shade

The reverse roll-up shade is a practical, tailored shade that covers the window frame and hangs from a rod inside a padded cornice. Decorative lining, fused to the shade fabric, rolls to the outside of the shade and is visible even when the shade is lowered to the sill. The shade is held in the rolled position by winding the cord around an awning cleat. Or a lock pulley can be used, allowing the draw cords to hang free. *Because of the cord loops, this style of shade is not recommended for a home with small children.*

Select two mediumweight, firmly woven fabrics that will bond well. Avoid fabrics with water-resistant or stain-resistant finishes which may prohibit bonding. Test a sample to be sure the fabrics bond securely. Hold the shade fabric and lining up to the light to check for pattern show-through.

Make and cover the cornice, following the instructions on pages 71 to 73.

✂ Cutting Directions

Cut shade fabric and fusible web 1" (2.5 cm) narrower than inside measurement of cornice and 12" (30.5 cm) longer than length from rod socket in cornice to sill. Cut lining 2" (5 cm) wider and 3½" (9 cm) longer than shade fabric. Cut two lengths of shade cord, 3 times the length of the shade plus width.

YOU WILL NEED

Shade fabric, contrasting solid lining, and paper-backed fusible web.

Covered cornice, inside measurements 5" (12.5 cm) deep and 4" (10 cm) wider than window frame.

Four screw eyes. Or three screw eyes and a lock pulley.

Utility rod with sockets, the same size as the inside cornice width.

One dowel, ½" (1.3 cm) diameter, width of finished shade; shade cord; awning cleat; drapery pull; angle irons for mounting.

Note: If shade is wider than 36" (91.5 cm), add another angle iron, shade cord, and two screw eyes for center of shade.

How to Sew a Reverse Roll-up Shade

1) Place shade *wrong* side up on large ironing surface. Place fusible web, paper side up, over shade, aligning edges. Fuse, following manufacturer's directions. Allow to cool; carefully remove paper.

2) Place lining wrong side up on ironing surface. Place shade over lining with fusible side down, 1½" (3.8 cm) from bottom, 2" (5 cm) from top; center from side to side. Fuse lining to shade, following manufacturer's directions. Allow to cool completely.

3) Press lining to right side in ½" (1.3 cm) double-fold side hems; stitch. Press ½" (1.3 cm), then 1½" (3.8 cm) to right side on upper edge. Press ½" (1.3 cm), then 1" (2.5 cm) to right side on lower edge. Stitch, forming rod pockets. Insert utility rod in upper pocket; insert dowel in lower pocket.

4) Mark center line along length of cornice top; insert screw eyes 2" (5 cm) on either side of center line and 6" (15 cm) in from ends. Or attach a lock pulley instead of front screw eye on draw side. Attach curtain rod sockets to the center of cornice ends.

5) Tie cord on draw side **(a)** to screw eye at back of cornice, and thread through corresponding screw eye or pulley at front. Repeat for second side **(b)**, bringing cord across top and threading through front screw eye or pulley on draw side. Mount cornice, using angle irons.

6) Attach awning cleat to side of window frame, if lock pulley is not used. Insert shade in sockets. Loop the cords around shade. Adjust cords so shade is level. Insert cord ends in drapery pull; knot ends.

Bishop Sleeve Curtains

These elegant pouffed curtains are simply rod pocket curtains with extra length allowed for blousing. The bishop sleeve look is achieved with tiebacks pulling the curtain tight to the window frame. Any number of poufs may be used. Arrange and tie the poufs at a position that is in proportion to the window length and width.

The poufs are balanced on each side of the tieback because the curtain rod extends 6" to 8" (15 to 20.5 cm) on each side of the window. If side space is limited, they may also hang straight on the outer edge, with the pouf draping only to the center of the window.

Tiebacks are tight on this curtain, in contrast to loose-fitting tiebacks on most curtain panels. For a decorative effect, use tasseled tiebacks or floppy bows with long streamers. Or use cord to tie the poufs so tiebacks do not show. As a finishing touch, the soft, flowing look of the bishop sleeve curtains can be repeated with a pouf valance (page 60).

✄ Cutting Directions

Cut panels 2 to 2½ times wider than finished width. To finished length, add 12" (30.5 cm) extra for each pouf and 12" (30.5 cm) more to puddle on the floor; add allowance for double top heading and rod pocket. Add 2" (5 cm) for double bottom hem if puddling on floor, or 8" (20.5 cm) for double bottom hem if curtains come to the floor.

YOU WILL NEED

Decorator fabric for curtains.

Tiebacks and cup hooks for each pouf.

Flat curtain rod or pole with elbows.

How to Sew a Bishop Sleeve Curtain

1) Turn under and stitch double 1" (2.5 cm) side hems. Turn under and stitch rod pocket and heading. Stitch double bottom hems.

2) Insert rod; hang and gather panels evenly. Determine location of poufs by tightly bunching the panel with your hands and lifting it to different positions until you find a pleasing proportion.

3) Mark tieback position. Attach cup hook behind pouf to hold tieback. Tissue paper can be tucked into the pouf to improve blousing if fabric does not have as much body as you would like.

Tent-flap Curtains

Stylish tent-flap curtains require a minimum amount of fabric and provide a tailored, uncluttered look. Choose two fabrics that complement each other for the outer fabric and the lining. The lining is just as important as the outer fabric.

✂ Cutting Directions

Cut each panel half the width of the mounting board plus return, plus 2" (5 cm) for seam allowances and overlap; cut length as measured from the top of the mounting board to desired finished length, plus the depth of the mounting board and ½" (1.3 cm) for seam allowance. Cut face fabric and lining panels the same size.

YOU WILL NEED

Decorator fabric and lining for curtains.

Mounting board: For outside mount, board should extend at least 1" (2.5 cm) on each side of window frame and be deep enough to clear window by 2" (5 cm). For inside mount, cut 1 × 2 to fit inside window.

Two tieback holders or two wooden blocks.

Two angle irons for mounting.

Heavy-duty stapler, staples.

How to Sew a Tent-flap Curtain

1) Pin face fabric to lining, right sides together, and stitch three sides in ½" (1.3 cm) seam, leaving upper edge open.

2) Press one seam allowance back to make it easier to turn a crisp, sharp edge. Trim seam allowance across corners. Turn panels right side out, and press.

3) Mark finished length across the top of the panels, making sure that both panels are exactly even and that end is at perfect right angle to sides.

4) Align panel length marking with front edge of mounting board. Staple panel to board, starting at return. At corner, make diagonal fold to form a miter. Panels overlap about 1" (2.5 cm) at center.

5) Mount board with angle irons positioned at edge of window frame.

6) Fold the front edges of the panels back to side edges, and adjust opening. Measure to be sure they are even on both sides.

7) Hand-tack two layers together, and finish with decorative or covered button. Or hand-tack ties at front edge and sides. To maintain projection at sides, attach panel to tieback holder or wooden block attached to window frame behind ties.

Inside mounting. Cut panels half the finished width of mounting board, plus 2" (5 cm). Sew as for steps 1 to 3. Mount panels on top of board. Fold flap; tack to side of curtain. At side, sew ring to curtain back; attach to cup hook inside frame.

Top Treatments

Top treatments give curtains, draperies, or shades a custom look that sets the window apart from the ordinary. They include valances, poufs, swags and jabots, and cornices. They may be used alone, to allow the maximum light or view through a window, or with any curtain or drapery to cover an unattractive rod, or simply as a decorative accent.

Top treatments are used not only with curtains and draperies, but also with shower curtains, mini-blinds, pleated shades, vertical blinds, and shutters to soften the overall appearance or to coordinate fabric or color within a room.

A top treatment can be a useful camouflage. It can help to extend the visual height of a window or can make it appear shorter, depending on the style and placement. Valances and cornices can make windows that are at different levels in a room appear uniform. When wall space is limited for drapery stackback, a top treatment used by itself can give the window a finished look without a great deal of effort.

Fabric has a lot to do with the look. The same style can be made in moiré or linen; the moiré will be elegant for a tailored look, and the linen will be more casual for a country look. A straight valance or cornice is usually more tailored than one that is gathered, but in a formal fabric a gathered one can be just as elegant.

Valances are simply short curtains, draperies, or soft shades used at the top of a window. A valance may be mounted on a separate curtain rod or on a mounting board inside or outside the window frame. Mounting boards are cut from 1" (2.5 cm) lumber; the depth may be 2" to 5" (5 to 12.5 cm), or more, depending on the return of the underdrapery, curtain, or shade. Valances are generally "soft," as opposed to a "hard" cornice constructed of plywood.

Pouf valances are variations of soft cloud or balloon shades, made by shirring fabric on two curtain rods. The *double pouf* valance uses three curtain rods. For deeper headings and taller windows, wider utility rods may also be used for pouf valances.

Swags are soft drapes of fabric across the top of the window. They are usually attached to a mounting board, although a more informal look is to drape a swag over a wooden or decorative pole. They usually have an attached side drape of fabric, called either a *jabot* or a *cascade*. Jabots may be pleated, gathered, or casually draped.

Cornices are custom-built boxes without backs that cover the top of the window. They may be stained, painted, or upholstered to match a window treatment. The lower edge of a cornice may be cut straight or cut into a decorative shape.

Measuring for a Top Treatment

There are few hard and fast rules for top treatments, because they are an excellent opportunity to express creativity. In general, the length of the valance should be in proportion to the total length of the window or window treatment. This length is usually about one-fifth of the window treatment. To add visual height to a room, a top treatment may be mounted at the ceiling, or at least several inches (centimeters) above the window.

For scalloped treatments such as the Austrian valance, the shortest point of the scallop should come 4" (10 cm) below the top of the window glass and cover 6" to 8" (15 to 20.5 cm) of an underdrapery heading.

If a valance or cornice is not mounted at the ceiling, allow at least 4" (10 cm) of clearance between the top of the drapery and the valance for the mounting brackets.

For mounting a top treatment over draperies, add 4" (10 cm) to the width, and 2" to 3" (5 to 7.5 cm) to the depth on each side, to allow for clearance at the return. For example, if using a valance with an underdrapery, use a 5½" (14 cm) valance return over a standard 3½" (9 cm) underdrapery return.

Pouf Valance

The pouf valance is shirred on two curtain rods to create a soft, gathered top treatment. It can be casual and relaxed in mediumweight prints, but creates an elegant look in a sheer fabric, especially when used over sheer curtains and draperies. This valance can also be mounted on two tension rods for use as a shower curtain valance.

If the valance is installed over draperies, the projection on the curtain rods should clear the draperies by at least 2" (5 cm). To make the valance stand away from the drapery, use rods that have at least 1" (2.5 cm) difference in the return. The deeper return may be used as the lower rod to clear a drapery, or the shorter return may be used as the lower rod to allow the fabric to pouf with a more natural flare.

Mount the lower rod up to half the length of the valance. For example, for a 14" (35.5 cm) valance install the lower rod about 7" (18 cm) below the upper rod. You may prefer to mount the lower rod after the valance is finished because every fabric will pouf differently.

✂ Cutting Directions

Cut valance 2½ to 3 times the finished width, and 2 times the estimated length from top of upper rod to lowest point of valance to allow enough fabric for rod pockets, double heading, and pouffing.

YOU WILL NEED

Decorator fabric for valance.

Two flat curtain rods with 1" (2.5 cm) difference in returns. Wide rod may be used for top rod.

How to Sew a Pouf Valance

1) Mount upper rod. To estimate length, drape a tape measure from the rod, down to the desired position, and back up to the lower rod position. (Lower rod has been mounted to show position.)

2) Seam widths of fabric together. Turn under and stitch double 1" (2.5 cm) side hems. Turn under ½" (1.3 cm), then allowance for rod pocket and heading. Stitch rod pocket and heading.

3) Turn under ½" (1.3 cm), then allowance for rod pocket on lower edge of valance; stitch. Insert curtain rods into rod pockets. Position and mount lower rod. Adjust poufs.

Double Pouf Valance

The double pouf is simply an extension of the pouf valance with an extra rod pocket stitched in the center. Three curtain rods are used for installation, with the middle rod mounted an equal distance from the upper and lower rods.

The double pouf can cover up to half the window. When used without an undercurtain, the valance can also be mounted on tension rods inside the window frame. Shutters or cafe curtains may be used on the lower half of the window.

The cut length does not have to be exact, because the fabric poufs and the distance between rods can be adjusted. If the fabric seems too limp and does not pouf as much as you would like, use lightly crumpled tissue paper in the poufs.

✂ Cutting Directions

Cut valance 2½ to 3 times the finished width, and 2 times the estimated length from top of upper rod to lowest point of valance to allow enough fabric for rod pockets, double heading, and pouffing.

YOU WILL NEED

Decorator fabric for valance.

Three flat curtain rods or tension rods.

How to Sew a Double Pouf Valance

1) Mount upper rod. Drape tape measure to estimate length of poufs and overall length of valance. (Lower and middle rods have been mounted to show position.)

2) Seam widths of fabric; stitch side hems, upper and lower rod pockets, and heading. Fold valance in half, right sides together; match upper and lower rod pockets. Stitch rod pocket 1½" (3.8 cm) from fold.

3) Insert curtain rods into rod pockets. Position and mount rods as desired. Adjust poufs.

Austrian Valance

The Austrian valance is a shortened version of the elegant Austrian shade, characterized by vertical rows of shirring, horizontal gathers, and soft scallops at the lower edge. Sheer and soft fabrics work best for this treatment, which is often trimmed with fringe. The valance is unlined to gather and drape beautifully.

There can be any number of scallops across the lower edge, but they are usually about 8" to 12" (20.5 to 30.5 cm) apart. This measurement may vary for wider or narrower windows. To determine the finished width of each scallop, divide the width of the mounting board by the number of scallops desired.

The directions that follow are for a valance mounted inside the window frame.

✂ Cutting Directions

Cut fabric 1½ times the width of mounting board and 2½ times the finished length. Cut sheer fabric 3 times the length. If it is necessary to seam widths together, position seams at shirring lines.

YOU WILL NEED

Decorator fabric for valance and, if desired, for mounting board.

Two-cord shirring tape, the cut length of valance (plus extra for finishing) times number of scallops, plus one.

1" (2.5 cm) twill tape, width of finished valance plus 1" (2.5 cm).

Optional trim, the cut width of the valance, plus extra for finishing.

Mounting board, 1 × 2; heavy-duty stapler, staples; tacks or pushpins.

Two angle irons for mounting.

Wooden dowel for weight rod, the finished width of valance.

How to Sew an Austrian Valance

1) **Seam** fabric if necessary for width. Press under 1½" (3.8 cm) on each side. For trim at lower edge, press ½" (1.3 cm) at bottom of curtain to *right* side. Pin heading of trim over raw edge; stitch. For valance without trim, stitch double 1" (2.5 cm) hem.

2) **Divide** cut width by number of scallops. For example, if the hemmed width is 72" (183 cm) and there are four scallops, the width of each scallop before shirring is 18" (46 cm). Mark at upper and lower edges.

3) **Pin** 2-cord shirring tape from lower to upper edge on each mark. Place tape 1" (2.5 cm) from sides to cover raw edges. Stitch both edges of tape in same direction.

4) **Tie** cords at bottom so they will not pull out; pull shirring tape cords from top, gathering all cords to the same finished length. Secure ends of cord with knot.

5) **Mark** mounting board to match *finished* width of scallops. Valance is wider than mounting board. Match tape to marks, and tack. Divide excess fabric evenly on each side of markings; pleat and pin in place.

6) **Remove** valance from mounting board. Stitch twill tape over raw edge to finish upper edge and to use for mounting.

7) **Staple** or tack twill tape to top of mounting board. Place staples 6" (15 cm) apart.

8) **Cover** wooden dowel with matching fabric. Hand-tack to back of valance at shirring lines.

Tapered Valance

The graceful curve of a tapered valance frames a window in soft folds of fabric. This valance is often used over mini-blinds and pleated shades to soften severe lines, or with short cafe curtains for a comfortable, casual look.

Tapered valances are usually lined when print fabrics are used, because you see the wrong side of the fabric as it cascades down the sides of the window. If the lower edge has a ruffled finish, however, it does not have to be lined because the fall of the ruffle hides the wrong side of the fabric. Lightweight or sheer fabrics are also good choices for a ruffled valance, and do not require a lining.

The side length can be to the sill or apron, but it should be no less than one-third the length of the window. To determine the finished length at center of valance, see Measuring for a Top Treatment, page 59. To check the curve, you may wish to make a paper pattern or mock-up with old sheets or lining fabric.

✂ Cutting Directions

Cut fabric and lining 2 times the width of the rod. To estimate length, measure at longest point and add amount for rod pocket and heading plus 1" (2.5 cm) for seam allowance and turn-under. To determine cut length at center of valance, add allowance for rod pocket and heading plus ½" (1.3 cm) for turn-under to desired finished length at center.

For unlined valance with ruffle, use 2½ times fullness for valance. Subtract width of ruffle from finished length. Cut ruffle 2 times the length of the curve and finished width plus 1" (2.5 cm); seam fabric as necessary. Measure the curve after cutting the valance; or make a test muslin, and measure.

YOU WILL NEED

Decorator fabric for valance.
Lining for valance.
Flat curtain rod or pole with elbows.

How to Sew a Tapered Valance

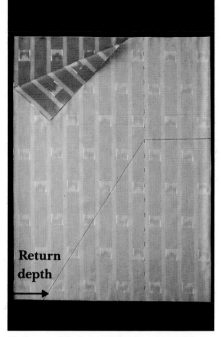

1) Seam fabric widths as necessary. Divide and mark fabric vertically into thirds. Fold in half. At center, mark cut length. At side, mark depth of return. Draw a straight line from return mark to nearest one-third marking at finished length in center.

2) Round upper corner into gentle curve; repeat for lower corner at return. Pin fabric layers together, and cut both layers as one. Center third is straight. Cut lining, using valance as pattern.

3) Place right side of lining and valance fabric together. Stitch ½" (1.3 cm) seam around valance, leaving upper edge open.

4) Press lining seam allowance toward lining. Clip curve. Diagonally trim corners.

5) Turn right side out. Turn under and stitch rod pocket and heading. Insert curtain rod in pocket.

Unlined valance with ruffle. Stitch 1" (2.5 cm) double side hems on valance. Turn under and stitch rod pocket and heading. Make and attach ruffle as on page 27.

Swags & Jabots

A classic *swag* is a draping of soft folds used as a top treatment with pleated or gathered side panels. The side panels of the treatment are the *jabots* or *cascades*.

Window width and personal preference determine the number of swags. Each swag should generally be no wider than 40" (102 cm). This size can be adapted to any window size by increasing or decreasing the overlap on adjoining swags, as shown on page 58. The length of a swag is usually from 15" to 20" (38 to 51 cm) at the longest point in the center. Shallower swags may be used on narrow windows.

The jabot length should be about one-third of the drapery or window length, or should fall to a point of interest, such as the sill or floor. Its shortest point should be lower than the center of the swag. Jabots are 9" to 11" (23 to 28 cm) wide. Pleated jabots are more formal than gathered jabots, which are less controlled. Instructions are given here for the pleated jabot, but cutting and sewing techniques are basically the same for a gathered jabot. To gather the jabot, zigzag over a cord and pull the cord up to the desired fullness.

For outside mounting, attach swags and jabots to a cornice or mounting board placed 4" (10 cm) above the molding if used alone, or about 4" (10 cm) above the drapery rod if they are used over draperies. The cornice return must be deep enough to clear the underdrapery. Jabot returns are the same width as the cornice or mounting board. In homes with beautiful moldings the swags may be mounted inside the window on a board that fits inside the frame, and there are no returns.

Make a test swag to use as a pattern for cutting the decorator fabric. Use muslin or an old sheet that will drape softly. The test swag provides an opportunity to experiment and determine the appearance you want. Do not hesitate to drape the muslin and pin it at different positions until you find the look you like.

For each jabot, you will need one width of decorator fabric and lining the length of the jabot plus 1" (2.5 cm). For each swag, you will need 1 yd. (.95 m) of decorator fabric and lining if draped tape measurement, left, is less than the fabric width; you will need 2 yd. (1.85 m) if draped measurement is more than the fabric width.

YOU WILL NEED

Muslin or an old sheet for test swag.

Decorator fabric and lining for swags and jabots.

Wide twill tape, width of the mounting board plus 2 times the return.

Mounting board or cornice; heavy-duty stapler.

How to Estimate the Size of a Swag

Drape a tape measure or string to simulate the planned shape of each swag. For double swags, drape two tape measures.

How to Cut Jabots and Swags

Jabots. Cut jabot 3 times finished width plus return and 1" (2.5 cm) seam allowance. On one side, mark shortest point plus 1" (2.5 cm). On the other side, mark longest point plus 1" (2.5 cm). From longest point, measure the width of return plus ½" (1.3 cm). Connect marks.

Swag. Cut muslin for the test swag 36" (91.5 cm) long. Cut the width the measurement from draped tape measure (left) plus 2" (5 cm) on each side for final adjustments. Mark width of window, centering marks at top of fabric. At lower edge, mark width from tape measure; connect the marks, forming diagonal guidelines. Divide each guideline equally into one more space than the number of folds; mark. For example, for five folds, divide into six spaces.

How to Make a Test Swag for Pattern

1) Fold muslin on first mark of diagonal line, and pull fold to the mark for upper corner; pin to ironing board. Continue pinning marked folds to corners, alternating sides and keeping upper edge straight.

2) Check the drape, and adjust pins and pleats as necessary. When folds are adjusted as desired, trim excess fabric 1" (2.5 cm) from outer edges and along the curved bottom edge about 3" (7.5 cm) from last fold.

3) Unpin folds. Fold in half lengthwise to check that it is balanced and even; adjust cutting lines. Use as a pattern for cutting swag and lining. Add ½" (1.3 cm) seam allowances on upper and lower edges. This swag is not finished on ends and is mounted under jabot.

Alternative style. Fold muslin at first marks, and bring fold up to mounting board about 5" (12.5 cm) from ends. Drape smoothly, and continue folding, pulling each fold up and out slightly, toward end of board. The swag is finished at ends and can be mounted on top of or under jabot.

How to Sew a Swag

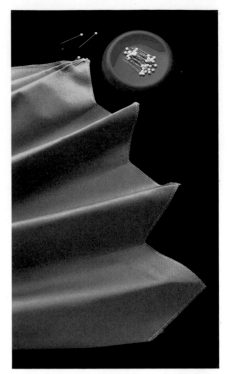

1) Pin lining to swag, right sides together, along lower curved edge. Stitch curved edge in ½" (1.3 cm) seam. Press lining seam allowance toward lining. Turn right side out; press stitched edge.

2) Pin swag front and lining together at remaining three sides. Overlock or zigzag raw edges together.

3) Pin pleats in place. The outside edge of each notch is the fold point.

4) Check drape of swag again by pinning swag to the side of ironing board or mounting board. Make minor adjustments as desired.

5) Stitch across all folds to hold pleats in place.

How to Sew Jabots

1) Place jabot lining and fabric, right sides together; stitch ½" (1.3 cm) seam on sides and bottom. Press lining seam allowance toward lining. Clip corners, and turn right side out. Press stitched edges. Stitch upper edges together in ½" (1.3 cm) seam. Zigzag or overlock raw edges.

2) Lay jabot, wrong side up, on large flat surface. On sides, fold under return and press in place. Turn jabot right side up.

3) Fold into evenly spaced pleats, starting on the outer edge; steam in position. Pleat other jabot in opposite direction. Check pleats by hanging jabot over edge of ironing board. Stitch ⅜" (1 cm) from upper edge to hold pleats in place.

How to Attach Swag and Jabots to a Mounting Board

1) Center swag on mounting board or cornice with edge of swag ½" (1.3 cm) from edge of board. Staple swag to board at 6" (15 cm) intervals.

2) Place top of one jabot at end of mounting board, with pressed fold at corner. Staple return in place. Position pleats on mounting board, overlapping swag. Fold under excess fabric at corner, and staple.

3) Cover fabric edges with wide twill tape. Staple tape along both edges, mitering at corners.

Padded Cornices

A cornice is a painted or fabric-covered wooden frame used as a tailored top treatment. When fabric-covered, the frame is padded with foam or bonded polyester to round the corners and give it a soft, upholstered look.

A cornice not only frames and finishes a window treatment by hiding the hardware, but also provides good insulation and energy-saving efficiency, because it encloses the top of the treatment and prevents cold air from escaping into the room.

Cornices are usually custom-built to fit the window. With simple carpentry skills you can build a cornice from plywood or pine boards. Any imperfections in the carpentry are covered with padding and fabric.

Measure the outside frame of the window after the drapery hardware is in place. The cornice should clear the curtain or drapery heading by 2" to 3" (5 to 7.5 cm), and it should extend at least 2" (5 cm) beyond the end of the drapery on each side. The measurements are the cornice *inside* measurements. Allow for the thickness of the wood when cutting.

The cornice should completely cover the drapery headings and hardware. Generally, apply the same guidelines for height as for any other top treatment. The cornice should be about one-fifth the height of the window treatment.

Use contrasting welting around the top and bottom edges to set the cornice apart when it is covered with the same fabric as the drapery.

Railroad the fabric on a cornice to eliminate seams on plain fabrics. If the fabric cannot be railroaded, place the seams inconspicuously, never in the center. Prints should be centered or balanced.

✄ Cutting Directions

For face piece, cut decorator fabric 6" (15 cm) wider than front plus sides, and the height of cornice plus 3" (7.5 cm). Cut a 4" (10 cm) inner lining strip from decorator fabric, the same width as the face piece. Cut a strip of lining fabric the same width as the face piece and 2" (5 cm) shorter than the cornice height. Cut fabric for dust cover 1" (2.5 cm) larger than cornice top.

Cut a strip of batting or foam to cover the front and sides of the cornice.

Cover cording, page 29, step 1, to make welting slightly longer than the distance to be welted.

YOU WILL NEED

Decorator fabric and lining to cover cornice; optional coordinating or contrasting fabric for welting.

To build the cornice, ½" (1.3 cm) plywood for the front, top, and sides; carpenter's glue; sixpenny finishing nails.

To pad the cornice, 1" (2.5 cm) bonded polyester upholstery batting or ½" (1.3 cm) foam. If not available in local stores, you may be able to obtain through an upholsterer or upholstery supply.

5⁄32" (3.8 mm) cording slightly longer than the distance to be welted.

Cardboard upholsterer's stripping to cover top and bottom edges; heavy-duty stapler, ½" (1.3 cm) and ¼" (6 mm) staples; spray foam adhesive; angle irons for mounting.

How to Build a Cornice

1) Measure and cut top to correspond to inside measurements for clearance. Cut front same width as top, and desired height. Cut sides same height as cornice and depth of top piece plus thickness of plywood.

2) Glue the top in place to front of board first. Remember which edges abut. Nail to secure. Then attach sides, first gluing in place to hold and then securing with nails.

How to Pad and Cover a Cornice

1) **Stitch** welting on right side of face piece in ½" (1.3 cm) seam, raw edges even. Sew welted edge to inner lining strip; sew free edge of inner strip to lining. Fold face piece in half to mark center at top and bottom.

2) **Mark** center of cornice at top and bottom. Place wrong side of face fabric on outside of cornice, with welting seam on lower front edge of cornice; match center markings. Tack.

3) **Pull** seam taut to corners, and tack. Staple every 4" (10 cm) from center to ends. Flip lining back to check that welting is straight.

4) **Place** cardboard stripping tight against welting seam. Staple every 1" to 1½" (2.5 to 3.8 cm). Cut and overlap stripping at corners.

5) **Fold** lining to inside. Fold under raw edge, and staple at inside where top and face meet; at lower corners, miter fabric and staple close to corner. Tuck excess fabric into upper corners, and staple.

6) **Rip** excess welting seam back to end of cornice; trim welting to 1" (2.5 cm). Trim cord even with cornice edge. Staple lining to wall end of cornice; trim excess lining. Staple welting to wall end.

7) Turn cornice face up. Apply adhesive to front and sides. Place padding over glued surface, and stretch it slightly toward each end. Allow glue to set.

8) Fold face fabric over the front of cornice. Use a screwdriver to hold padding in place at corners. Gently smooth fabric toward top of cornice.

9) Tack at center and ends, removing slack. Do not stretch too tightly. Starting at center, turn under raw edge and staple to each end, placing staples 1½" (3.8 cm) apart, smoothing fabric as you go.

10) Pull fabric around corner to top back corner, removing slack; tack. Fold side fabric to back edge; staple. Trim excess fabric at back edge.

11) Fold fabric diagonally at corner to form a miter. Staple at corner and across ends. If fabric is bulky, tap staple with hammer. Repeat on both corners.

Welting at upper edge. Staple welting to sides and front, with seam at edge. On cornice front, place dust cover over welting, with right sides together and raw edges even. Staple cardboard stripping at front and side edges as in step 4, opposite. Pull fabric to top of cornice, and fold under at sides and back; staple next to folds.

Bed & Bath

Sewing for the Bedroom & Bath

The bedroom and bath are often thought of together because of the fabric and color coordination. It is also a good area to try your hand at sewing projects because the typical fabrics for these rooms are easy to work with. Although a spread, comforter, or shower curtain may be bulky to handle, there are few measurements to take and the straight seaming and hems are simple to sew.

Start with a shower curtain and a coordinated valance. A sink skirt and embellished towels complete the look. Consider sewing a duvet cover for a comforter, with a coordinated dust skirt and shams. Shirring on upper and lower edges gives a custom look to the dust skirt. The same technique can be used, on a smaller scale, as a border on the pillow sham. As a finishing touch, sew a swagged table topper or a fabric screen. For a guest bedroom, sew a custom cover for a futon.

Measuring the Bed

Measure the bed with the blankets and sheets that are normally on the bed. This may make the measurements larger than the actual mattress size, but it will ensure that the bedcover is not skimpy and that fitted covers fit the bed perfectly.

Measure from side to side across the top of the mattress for width, and from the head to the foot of the bed for length.

Comforters, coverlets, and duvets reach 3" to 4" (7.5 to 10 cm) below the mattress on two sides and at the foot of the bed. The drop length is the distance from the upper edge of the mattress to the bottom of the comforter, usually 9" to 12" (23 to 30.5 cm), depending on the depth of the mattress.

For dust skirt length, measure from the top of the box spring to the floor.

To determine how many widths of fabric are needed, divide the total width of the bedcover by the fabric width; round off to the next highest number. Most bedcovers, require two or three fabric widths. Multiply the number of widths by the length of the bedcover for amount of fabric needed. Divide by 36" (100 cm) to determine the number of yards (meters).

For most bedcovers you will need to seam the panels together. Cut one full width for the center and two equal, partial-width panels for each side. If the fabric has a large print motif, be sure to allow extra fabric for matching at seams.

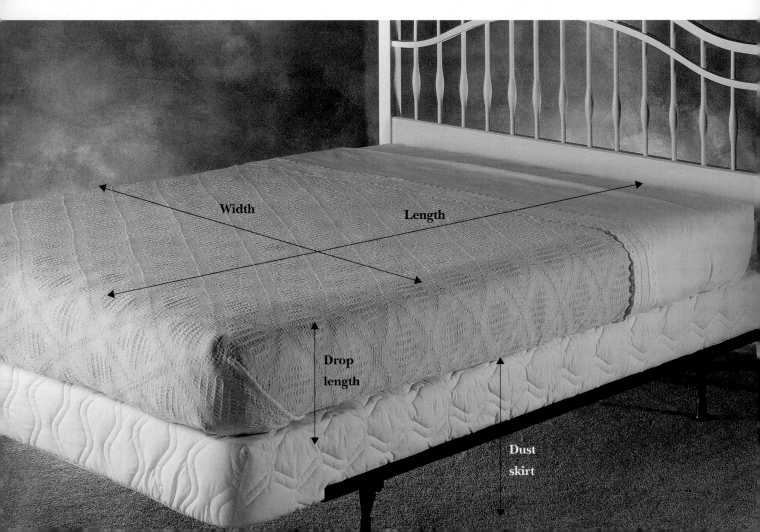

Width

Length

Drop length

Dust skirt

Sewing with Sheets

Sheets are practical for duvet covers because their width makes seaming and matching unnecessary, but they are not always printed on-grain, and the design does not match at the selvage as with decorator fabrics. If all four sides of the sheet are hemmed, the sheet may have been cut on the crosswise, instead of lengthwise, grain. Consider the grainline before tearing or cutting sheets.

The sizes given below are general guidelines to use in determining how many sheets will be needed for the duvet or comforter cover. Comforters and sheets may vary in size, especially after laundering. Preshrink all-cotton sheets and flannel sheets before cutting.

Except for a crib-size cover, which can be made from one twin-size sheet, you will need two appropriately sized sheets for the comforter or duvet cover. There will be enough fabric left on the sides of the two sheets to cut welting strips. Use an extra flat sheet to trim the duvet with a self-ruffle.

Sheet Requirements for Duvet Covers

Bed Size	Sheets for Duvet Cover	Sheets for 4" (10 cm) Self-ruffle	Number of 1½" (3.2 cm) Welting Strips	Standard Duvet Sizes
Crib	1 twin flat	1 twin flat	3 lengthwise strips	42" × 52" (107 × 132 cm)
Bunk	2 twin flat	1 twin flat	5 lengthwise strips	59" × 82" (150 × 208 cm)
Twin	2 twin flat	1 twin flat	5 lengthwise strips	68" × 86" (173 × 218 cm)
Full	2 full flat	1 twin flat	5 lengthwise strips	76" × 86" (193 × 218 cm)
Queen	2 queen flat	1 full flat	5 lengthwise strips	86" × 86" (218 × 218 cm)
King	2 king flat	1 full flat	4 lengthwise strips	101" × 86" (257 × 218 cm)

Squaring Corners of Sheets

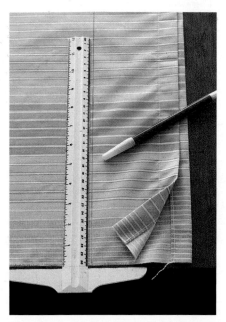

Determine direction of grain. To determine lengthwise grain, hold a section of sheet and pull in both directions. The direction with the least amount of stretch is the lengthwise grain.

Tear on lengthwise grain only. Measure from selvage, and tear along *lengthwise* grain for width. If you tear on crosswise grain, you will not get squared right angles.

Cut on crosswise grain. Fold sheet in half lengthwise so it lies smooth with no twist; line up edges of fabric with table edge. Use a T-square to mark length. Cut with rotary cutter or shears.

Duvet Covers

A duvet is a plump comforter or continental quilt, puffed with down or fiberfill. To change the look of an existing comforter or to protect a muslin-colored duvet, sew a duvet cover. This cover is similar to a large pillowcase with a hidden zipper in the back so the cover can be easily removed for laundering.

Duvet covers are easier to sew than full-size bedspreads because they do not require as much fabric and are therefore not as bulky to handle. Sheets are an ideal fabric choice because they do not require seaming for full widths, and when used on the bed they do not require an additional top sheet. Even if you are not using sheets for the entire cover, you can use a sheet for the back of the duvet.

These covers also lend themselves to the use of decorative touches such as a ruffle on all edges, contrasting welting in the seam, or both. Tucks, applied decorative stripes, lace, or an appliqué may be stitched on the top.

✂ Cutting Directions

Measure the down or fiberfill duvet. For a snug fit, make the finished duvet cover 2" (5 cm) shorter and 2" (5 cm) narrower than duvet measurements.

Cut front 1" (2.5 cm) wider and 1" (2.5 cm) longer than finished size; cut the back the same width and 1½" (3.8 cm) shorter than the front. Cut zipper strip 3½" (9 cm) wide and the same length as the cut width of the back.

For welting, cut fabric strips 1½" (3.8 cm) wide and 2 times the length and 2 times the width of the duvet, plus a few inches extra for finishing. Cut ⁵⁄₃₂" (3.8 mm) cording the same length as fabric strips.

For a 4" (10 cm) self-ruffle, cut fabric strips 9" (23 cm) wide. Join as necessary to get a strip that is 4 times the length plus 4 times the width of the duvet. For an eyelet ruffle, cut 4" to 6" (10 to 15 cm) eyelet edging 4 times the length plus 4 times the width. For pregathered eyelet trim, cut trim 2 times the length plus 2 times the width.

YOU WILL NEED

Flat sheets or washable cotton or cotton/polyester fabric for front and back. If using sheets, see page 77 for number of sheets needed. For fabric, measure bed and determine amount needed as on page 76.

Two zippers, 22" (56 cm) long.

Optional ⁵⁄₃₂" (3.8 mm) cording, ruffling, or self-ruffling.

How to Sew a Duvet Cover with Welting

1) Make welting as in step 1, page 29. Stitch to right side of front, matching raw edges. Clip and ease welting at corners. Join ends as in steps 3 to 5, page 29.

2) Overlock or zigzag upper edge of zipper strip and lower edge of the back. Press the finished edge of zipper strip under ½" (1.3 cm), and the finished edge of back under 1" (2.5 cm).

3) Place closed zippers facedown on seam allowance of back, with tabs meeting in center and edge of zipper tapes on fold. Using zipper foot, stitch one side of zippers.

4) Turn right side up; place pressed edge of zipper strip along edge of teeth on other side of zippers, and stitch close to edge. Backstitch at end of zippers.

5) Stitch across the end of the zippers; then topstitch through all layers to close the seam from the end of the zippers to the side edges. Open the zippers.

6) Pin duvet front to back, right sides together. With front side up, stitch, using zipper foot; crowd stitches close to first stitching. Turn duvet cover right side out, and insert duvet.

How to Sew a Ruffled Duvet Cover

1) Join ends of ruffling strips to form circle. Fold in half lengthwise, right side out. Zigzag raw edges together ¼" (6 mm) from edge, using longest and widest stitch. Divide into four equal sections, and mark with safety pins; also mark center of each side of front.

2) Use ruffler attachment or shirring foot, set for double fullness, to gather ruffle ⅜" (1 cm) from edge. Test on a scrap. It is easier to ruffle a little less than 2 to 1 and ease in gathers than to ruffle more tightly and have to clip threads, which may result in flat sections between gathers.

3) Match safety pins on ruffle to marks on front section. Pin and machine-baste ruffle to front, stitching just inside gathering row. Ease some extra fullness into ruffle at corners, so ruffle lies flat when turned to right side.

4) Insert the zipper, following steps 2 to 5 for cover with welting, page 79.

5) Pin front to back, right sides together. With front side up, stitch ½" (1.3 cm) from edges. Turn cover right side out, and insert duvet.

How to Sew a Duvet Cover with Ruffle and Welting

1) Follow steps 1 to 5 for cover with welting (page 79) and steps 1 and 2, opposite, for ruffled cover.

2) Pin and machine-baste ruffle to front over welting. Match ruffle to front, and ease in fullness as in step 3, above. Finish as in step 5, above; stitch, crowding welting.

Tuck-pleated Dust Skirt

A fitted lining holds the tuck-pleated dust skirt in place. Although the skirt gives an upholstered look, the four corners are split to fit over the bed frame, then held together with short strips of hook and loop tape. The tape is attached to grosgrain ribbon that is sewn into the seam.

✂ Cutting Directions

If using a sheet or a fabric that lends itself to tearing, tear along the lengthwise grain to obtain strips the desired drop plus 1" (2.5 cm) for seam allowances; join strips together to make one strip 2 times the width and 4 times the length of bed, plus 40" (102 cm) for extensions at head of the bed.

For deck, cut flat sheet 1" (2.5 cm) wider and 1" (2.5 cm) longer than box spring.

Cut lining the same drop as the skirt; cut two pieces the length of box spring, and one piece the width of box spring; cut two extensions to wrap around the head of the bed 11" (28 cm) long.

Cut welting strips 1½" (3.8 cm) wide, and 2 times the length plus 2 times the width of the deck. Cut 5/32" (3.8 mm) cording the same length as welting strips.

Cut 8 pieces of grosgrain and 8 pieces of hook and loop tape 2" (5 cm) long.

YOU WILL NEED

Decorator fabric or sheet for dust skirt on three sides of bed plus extensions.

Flat sheets for deck and lining.

Grosgrain ribbon, 1½" (3.8 cm) wide.

Hook and loop tape.

5/32" (3.8 mm) cording for welting.

How to Sew a Tuck-pleated Dust Skirt

1) Fold deck in half lengthwise, then crosswise so all four cut or torn corners are together. Using a saucer for a guide, cut through all layers to curve corners gently.

2) Fold curved corners in half to determine centers; mark fold with ¼" (6 mm) clip through all layers.

3) Tuck-pleat skirt ⅜" (1 cm) from upper and lower edges, using ruffler attachment set at 2 to 1 fullness; keep right side of fabric up.

4) **Make** welting, page 29, step 1; machine-baste welting to lower edge of pleated skirt and around deck edge, matching raw edges. Steam press to lightly flatten tucks.

5) **Cut** lengths of pleated skirt to match lining pieces. Release a few pleats if necessary to flatten skirt for 1" (2.5 cm) at each end. Square and trim ends to match lining.

6) **Cut** ½" (1.3 cm) of cording out of ends of welting. Fold welting back on itself, and pin to square and finish ends.

7) **Attach** loop side of hook and loop tape to ends of long lining pieces; sew one strip ½" (1.3 cm) from raw edge and ½" (1.3 cm) from bottom, and second strip ½" (1.3 cm) from raw edge and in center of side.

8) **Stitch** hook side of hook and loop tape on grosgrain strips, ½" (1.3 cm) from edge. Stitch strips on remaining pieces of skirt, matching the tapes that were stitched in step 7.

9) **Stitch** lower and side edges of skirt to lining, right sides together. Turn skirt right side out, and machine-baste top edges of skirt to lining ⅜" (1 cm) from edge. Do not trim grosgrain ribbon.

10) **Stitch** upper edge of skirt sections to deck edges, right sides together. Skirt sections with tape extensions underlap adjacent section ¼" (6 mm) at corners. Serge or zigzag raw edges together.

How to Sew a Tuck-pleated Pillow Sham

1) Insert zipper in back of sham, following instructions for zipper insertion in duvet, page 79, steps 2 to 5. Cover cording and machine-baste to right side of back, matching raw edges; join ends of welting (page 29).

2) Tuck-pleat the border strip, ⅜" (1 cm) from both edges, using ruffler attachment at 2 to 1 ratio. Keep fabric same side up when pleating. Steam press finished strip lightly to flatten tucks.

3) Cut two strips 1" (2.5 cm) longer than finished sham length, and two strips 1" (2.5 cm) longer than finished sham width. On wrong side of short strips, fold corner back; mark width of strip with pin. Unfold; mark stitching angle from pin to corner.

Tuck-pleated Pillow Sham

The mitered, tuck-pleated border on this sham is a narrow version of the tuck-pleated dust skirt. The finished sham should be the same size as the pillow.

Cutting Directions

Cut the back 1" (2.5 cm) wider and 1½" (3.8 cm) shorter than the finished size. Cut a back zipper strip the same width as the back and 3½" (9 cm) wide. Cut the center of the front 4" (10 cm) narrower and shorter than finished sham; cut border strips 3½" (9 cm) wide and 4 times the length and width of the sham, plus extra for seaming strips.

For welting, cut strips 1½" (3.8 cm) wide and 2 times the length and 2 times the width of sham, plus extra for seaming.

YOU WILL NEED

Decorator fabric or sheets for sham.

Contrasting border fabric.

⁵⁄₃₂" (3.8 mm) **cording** for welting.

Zipper, 22" (56 cm) long.

4) Pin each marked strip to an unmarked strip, and stitch from corner to ½" (1.3 cm) from raw edge; backstitch. Trim seams to ¼" (6 mm), and press open.

5) Pin inner edges of border to sham front; stitch one side at a time, backstitching (arrow) at both ends of seam.

6) Pin front to back, right sides together; stitch ½" (1.3 cm) from edge on all four sides. To finish, overlock or zigzag raw edges. Turn to right side; insert pillow.

Duvet Cover from Sheets

To use the decorative border on a sheet, conceal the zippered opening under the border on the right side of the cover. Or add a decorative border to a plain sheet, using lace or ribbon trims.

✂ Cutting Directions

Measure the down or fiberfill duvet. For snug fit, make the finished duvet cover 2" (5 cm) shorter and 2" (5 cm) narrower than duvet measurements.

For back of cover, cut or tear a sheet 1" (2.5 cm) wider and 1" (2.5 cm) longer than finished size.

For front, cut or tear bordered sheet 1" (2.5 cm) wider than finished size; for bordered zipper flap, right, fold sheet in half lengthwise and mark a line 20" (51 cm) from edge of sheet; for zipper strip, mark second line 3" (7.5 cm) from first line. Cut on both lines. To determine the length to cut the remaining front section, use chart at right. Line up sheet section with edge of table, and use a T-square to square lower edge.

Cut Length of Duvet Cover Front	in. (cm)
1) Finished length of cover	
2) Bordered zipper flap, 20" (51 cm)	–
3) Width of border	+
4) 1" (2.5 cm) seam allowance	+
5) Front cut length	=

YOU WILL NEED

Flat sheets with decorative border. See page 77 for number and size of sheets.

Two zippers, 22" (56 cm) long.

How to a Sew a Duvet Cover from Sheets

1) Zigzag or overedge raw edges of zipper strip and upper edge of front. Pin zipper strip to upper edge, right sides together. Mark zipper opening 22" (56 cm) in both directions from center.

2) Stitch 1" (2.5 cm) zipper seam, starting at one side. At zipper marking, backstitch, and then machine-baste across zipper opening; backstitch and continue to other edge. Press seam open.

3) Center open zippers facedown on seam allowance, with teeth on basted seam and tab ends meeting in center. Using zipper foot, stitch on one side of teeth. Close zippers; stitch other side. Remove basting.

4) Pin decorative border section over zipper, right side up, with zipper seam 1" (2.5 cm) from inner edge of border. Stitch on edge of border through all layers. Open zippers.

5) Pin front to back, with right sides together and back side up. Stitch ½" (1.3 cm) from raw edge. To finish, serge or zigzag raw edges. Turn right side out; insert duvet.

How to Sew a Reverse Sham Bedcover

1) Fold face fabric and lining in half lengthwise. To round the corners at the foot of the cover and the top of the sham, line up corners evenly and use a saucer to mark curve. Cut on marked line.

2) Fold the bias strip in half lengthwise, wrong sides together; press. Stitch strip to right side of cover and sham, along curved edges, stitching a scant ½" (1.3 cm) from edge. Ease strip around curves so it lies smooth when turned.

3) Pin lining to face fabric on both sections, right sides together in ½" (1.3 cm) seam; stitch around cover, leaving upper edges open. Clip the curves, and turn both sections right side out.

Reverse Sham Bedcover

The reverse sham bedcover is an all-in-one cover for bed and pillows. It has an extra-deep flap at the top to fold back over the bed pillows, making the bed especially quick and easy to make.

The reverse sham technique can be adapted for duvets or full-size bedspreads. It also works as a sheet-weight bedcover for summer sleeping.

For a tailored feeling, without the look of separate pillow shams, add the sham extension to a duvet cover. Follow the instructions for a duvet cover (pages 78 to 79), leaving the upper edge open. Make the sham, and attach it as shown, below.

For versatility, use coordinating fabrics or sheets for the face and the lining, and make the cover reversible. The edges are finished with a flat bias trim.

✂ Cutting Directions

Seam panels together as necessary for width. For the cover, cut the face fabric and lining the width of the bed, plus 2 times the drop plus 1" (2.5 cm) seam allowance; cut the length the length of bed plus one drop, plus 1" (2.5 cm) for seam allowance.

For the sham, cut the face fabric and lining 28" (71 cm) deep and the same width as the cut width of the cover. This size is suitable for an average 20" (51 cm) pillow. For larger or smaller pillows, loosely measure over the curve of the pillow and add 1" (2.5 cm) for seam allowance. Cut sham in same direction as cover, matching stripes or motifs.

For trim, cut 2" (5 cm) bias strips of contrasting fabric 2 times the finished length plus 2 times the finished width, plus extra for seam allowances.

YOU WILL NEED

Decorator fabric and lining for bedcover.
Contrasting fabric for bias trim.

4) Bastestitch raw edges together across open ends of cover and sham. To stitch concealed French seam, match *wrong* side of sham to *right* side of cover. Stitch ¼" (6 mm) seam; press. Trim, turn, press, and stitch ⅜" (1 cm) from fold.

4a) Alternative seam. Match *right* side of sham to *wrong* side of cover, and stitch ½" (1.3 cm) seam; trim. Finish seam with zigzag or overlock stitch, or apply tricot bias binding.

5) Place cover on bed with pillows on top of cover. Fold reverse sham back over pillows. Seam is inside when sham is turned back.

Futon Covers

A futon is an affordable piece of multifunction furniture that can easily be converted from a chair or sofa to a bed by changing the position of the futon frame from an upright to a reclining position. Futon mattresses are available in the same sizes as regular bed mattresses, from crib size to California king, and in various thicknesses and qualities.

A futon cover is not only decorative, but also protects the futon mattress from becoming stained or worn. You can sew your own futon cover that coordinates with the decorating scheme of the room. For an affordable cover with fewer seams, use bed sheets instead of decorator fabric. Select a solid-colored sheet or a patterned sheet with a nondirectional design; this allows you to turn the mattress regularly with the cover on, maintaining even wear on the cover as well as the mattress. For durability, purchase 100 percent cotton sheets with a high thread count. Two sheets sized the same as the mattress provide enough fabric for the cover, including the front, back, and boxing strip; for example, two full-size sheets make a cover for a full-size mattress. Before you cut the pieces for the futon cover, remove the stitching from the hems. Then launder and press the sheets.

Make the cover so the length of the sheet, or the lengthwise grain, runs from the seat to the back, rather than from arm to arm, when the futon is used as a sofa or chair. If you choose to substitute a decorator fabric for the sheets, the seams will also run from the seat to the back.

For ease in inserting or removing the mattress, the cover is constructed with a zippered closure that extends along three sides. Custom-sized zippers are available from upholstery shops and many fabric stores, where the zipper tape is cut to the necessary length.

✂ Cutting Directions

As shown at right, determine the desired finished width of the boxing strip (a), equal to the thickness of the mattress; pin-mark on opposite sides of the mattress. Measure across the mattress, between pin marks, to determine the finished width of the futon cover (b). Repeat to determine finished length of the futon cover (c).

Cut the front and back pieces for the futon cover, with the length and width of the pieces 1" (2.5 cm)

longer and wider than the finished width and length of the futon cover.

Cut one piece for the boxing strip, with the cut length 1" (2.5 cm) longer than the length of the futon cover; the cut width is 1" (2.5 cm) wider than the finished width of the boxing strip. Cut one zipper tab, 4" (10 cm) long, with the cut width of the tab equal to the cut width of the boxing strip.

For the zippered boxing on one long side of the cover, cut two zipper strips, with the length of the strips 1" (2.5 cm) longer than the finished length of the mattress; the cut width of the zipper strips is 1¼" (3.2 cm) wider than one-half the finished width of the boxing strip. For the zippered boxing on the short sides of the cover, cut four zipper strips, with the length of the strips 1" (2.5 cm) longer than the finished width of the mattress; the cut width of the zipper strips is 1¼" (2.5 cm) wider than one-half the finished width of the boxing strip.

YOU WILL NEED

Decorator fabric or cotton sheets.

Zipper, with the length of the zipper tape equal to combined length of the top, bottom, and one side of mattress plus 1" (2.5 cm).

How to Sew a Futon Cover

1) Stitch one short zipper strip to each end of one long zipper strip in ½" (1.3 cm) seams, right sides together; start stitching at the raw edge and stop ½" (1.3 cm) from the opposite raw edge. Finish seams, using overlock or zigzag stitch; press open. Repeat, using remaining short and long zipper strips.

2) Place the zipper strips right sides together, matching the raw edges and seams. Machine-baste ¾" (2 cm) from the long edge where stitching of the end seams extends to the raw edge. Finish seams; press open.

3) Fold the strip in half, right sides together, with one seam allowance extending. Place the closed zipper facedown over seam allowances, with the teeth centered on the seamline and ends of the zipper tape even with ends of strip. Machine-baste zipper tape to the extended seam allowance.

4) Unfold strip. On right side, center a strip of ¾" (2 cm) transparent tape over seamline. Stitch on both sides of tape, securing the zipper. Remove tape and basting stitches.

5) Press the zipper tab in half, with wrong sides together. Open the zipper about 2" (5 cm). At the top end of zipper, place the tab over the zipper strip, right sides up; stitch across the end, a scant ½" (1.3 cm) from the raw edges, stitching carefully over the zipper teeth.

6) Stitch ends of the boxing strip to ends of the zipper strip, right sides together, stitching ½" (1.3 cm) seams; start and stop ½" (1.3 cm) from raw edges. Finish seams; press open.

7) Pin the boxing strip to the futon cover front, right sides together, matching seams to corners. With boxing strip faceup, stitch ½" (1.3 cm) seam, pivoting at corners.

8) Pin the opposite side of boxing strip to the futon cover back, right sides together, matching seams to corners; stitch. Finish remaining seams.

9) Open the zipper; turn the futon cover right side out. Insert the futon mattress; close the zipper, hiding the zipper pull under the tab.

Fabric Screen

Fabric screens are decorative and functional. A simple screen instantly blocks an unattractive view, fills an empty corner, or separates a conversation or sleeping area. It is also an elegant way to show off an unusual fabric.

Decorative folding screens with removable dowels for mounting fabric panels are available at stores selling unfinished furniture, or you may construct wooden frame panels and hinge them together.

If the fabric has no obvious right or wrong side, such as lace and a woven plaid or stripe, it can simply be hemmed on the sides. Fabrics with an obvious right and wrong side need to be made double or with a contrasting lining, because both sides of the fabric may show.

✂ Cutting Directions

For hemmed panels, measure from top of upper dowel to bottom of lower dowel; add allowance for rod pockets and double headings at the top and bottom. The rod pocket is 2 times the diameter of the dowel.

The cut width of the fabric panel depends on the fabric. Generally, 1½ times the fullness is sufficient and will not distort a print; add 2" (5 cm) to each panel for side hems. Small prints and solids may use more fullness.

For a lined panel, measure from the top of the upper heading to the bottom of the lower heading. Add 1" (2.5 cm) for seam allowances. Cut decorator fabric and lining same size.

YOU WILL NEED

Folding screen with removable dowels for fabric insertion.

Decorator fabric and optional lining, as determined by type of fabric.

How to Sew a Fabric Screen

1) Press under double ½" (1.3 cm) side hems; stitch. On ends, turn under ½" (1.3 cm), then heading and rod-pocket allowance. Stitch rod pockets and headings.

2) Slip the dowels into the rod pockets; attach panels to the screen.

How to Sew a Lined Fabric Screen

1) Pin right sides of decorator fabric and lining together with all edges even. On the lining, mark the heading and opening for rod pocket, allowing for ½" (1.3 cm) seam at upper and lower edges.

2) Stitch all four sides in ½" (1.3 cm) seam, leaving openings for upper and lower rod pockets on both sides of panel. Leave an 8" (20.5 cm) opening at lower edge for turning right side out.

3) Trim corners diagonally. Press lining seam allowances toward lining. Turn panel right side out. Press edges.

4) Stitch rod pockets on upper and lower edges, stitching across panel at opening. Edgestitch the 8" (20.5 cm) opening closed at the lower edge. Slip dowels into rod pockets; attach panels to screen.

Swagged Table Topper

To give basic round tablecloths a custom look, layer them in pairs. Make the bottom cloth floor length and the top cloth shorter. Although the length of the top cloth is not critical, cutting it one-third or two-thirds of floor length creates a pleasing proportion. For a standard table 30" (76 cm) high, the top cloth should end either 10" (25.5 cm) or 20" (51 cm) from the floor.

Shirr the upper cloth into graceful swags. To decide the number of swags and the depth to shirr the edge, layer the cloths on the table and pin some test swags in place.

For the fastest hem finish, use a serger to finish the edge or to make a rolled hem. On a conventional machine, apply bias binding and turn under a narrow hem.

YOU WILL NEED

Decorator fabric for table topper.

Strips of bias tricot or bias tape, equal to number of swags, each as long as the area to be shirred.

Narrow cords such as soutache braid or shade cord, cut twice as long as the area to be shirred plus 1" (2.5 cm). Number should equal the number of swags.

How to Sew a Swagged Table Topper

1) Fold hemmed round cloth into quarters, sixths, or eighths, depending on the number of swags. Press crease at each fold to mark desired depth of shirring.

2) Pin doubled cord at hem at each crease. Center bias tricot or bias tape over crease, and pin. Stitch through center of tape, catching cord in stitching at hem edge.

3) Bring cord next to stitching at center of tape. Using zipper foot, stitch along both outer edges of tape to encase cord.

4) Pull up cords to create swags. Adjust gathers, and tie ends of cords securely. Tuck ends of cord into swag; do not cut. Swags can be released for laundry or storage.

How to Sew a Sink or Vanity Skirt

1) Turn under and stitch double 1" (2.5 cm) hem on bottom edge. Turn under double 1" (2.5 cm) hem on center front edges. For 2-piece skirt, stitch narrow hem on back edges.

2) Press under 1" (2.5 cm) on upper edge of panels. Turn under raw edges on ends of shirring tape; pull out shirring cords. Place tape, right side up, over raw edge, with upper edge of tape ¼" (6 mm) from fold. Stitch both sides of tape.

3) Tie cords at both ends of shirring tape. From wrong side of skirt, pull up cords in shirring tape to the finished width. Knot cords; wrap and tuck under skirt. Adjust the gathers evenly.

Sink & Vanity Skirts

For covering up an outdated sink or bringing more fabric coordination into the bathroom, the sink skirt is a perennial favorite. It conceals the plumbing and provides a hidden storage area.

Vanity skirts are sewn the same way as the sink skirt. They can transform an unsightly table into a charming bedroom or bath accessory.

Self-styling shirring tapes, available in a variety of styles, make the sewing quick and easy and add a dimensional interest to the top of the skirt. For a more traditional approach, gather the upper edge (page 26). Attach the skirt to the sink or vanity with hook and loop tape so the skirt can easily be removed for laundering or a quick change. To make the skirt washable, hand-sew the tape in place.

If the sink skirt is attached on the outside porcelain, make two side panels; each panel of the skirt will extend from the center front to the wall. If the skirt is attached underneath the apron of the sink, it can be made in one piece with a center front opening.

✂ Cutting Directions

To finished length, add 3" (7.5 cm) for a double 1" (2.5 cm) bottom hem and 1" (2.5 cm) to turn under at the top. To determine cut width, measure the distance around the sink or vanity where the skirt will be attached; multiply by 2½ times the fullness. Add 4" (10 cm) for front opening hems.

Cut the number of panels as figured above, and seam together for width as needed. If necessary to seam extra widths, place seams toward back.

YOU WILL NEED

Decorator fabric for skirt.

Shirring tape the cut width of the upper edge of the flat panels before gathering.

Adhesive-backed hook and loop tape to go around the sink or vanity.

4) Finger press loop side of self-adhesive hook and loop tape to the wrong side of the skirt, over the shirring tape.

5) Attach the hook side of self-adhesive tape to the outside of the sink or vanity table. Attach skirt to tape.

Alternative mounting. To hang skirt under apron of sink, attach loop side of tape on right side of skirt ½" (1.3 cm) from upper edge; adhere the hook side of tape to underside of the sink. Attach skirt.

Embellished Towels

Perk up the bath with designer touches added to inexpensive, plain towels. Laces, ribbons, or monograms can be added to coordinate with bedroom sheets and trims, window treatments, and shower curtains.

Preshrink or steam-shrink woven ribbon trims, particularly all-cotton trims; polyester laces will not need preshrinking. Mark trimming placement on towel with water-soluble marking pen.

When applying trims to terry towels, loosen the tension and use a long stitch length. Ease the trimming slightly as you stitch; when the towel is folded on the rack, the trim will lie smooth.

Lace and ribbon. Trim towels with prefinished lace beading **(1)**, lace edging **(2)**, or galloon lace **(3)**. For lace beading, insert ribbon into beading, position beading on towel, and straight-stitch upper edge. For lace edging, position so lower edge of lace covers towel fringe or hem. Cover upper edge of lace with ribbon trim; straight-stitch along both edges of ribbon. For galloon lace, position trim on towel, and straight-stitch near edges of lace.

Machine monogram. On electronic sewing machine, insert monogram cassette and program desired lettering. Cover monogram area with dissolvable plastic film protector to prevent snagging terry loops. Stitch; tear away plastic film. Laundering dissolves any remaining film.

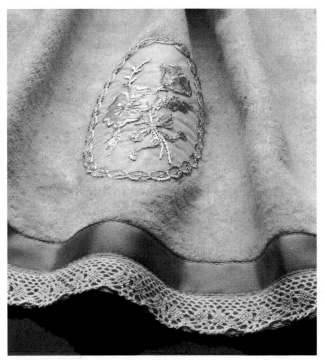

Lace motif. Cut single motif from Cluny or Venice lace, or use purchased appliqué. Fusible web may be used to hold appliqué in place; stitch with narrow zigzag. Coordinating trims may be stitched at lower edge of towel.

Shower Curtains

A simple shower curtain can instantly change and refresh a bathroom. Use the shower curtain as a bold splash of color. Coordinate window treatments, towels, and other accessories with your new shower curtain.

The shower curtain pictured, used with a plastic liner, is especially easy to sew because it does not require grommets or eyelets in the heading. Instead, use a drapery folding or pleating tape, and insert metal shower curtain hooks in the loops that are woven right into the tape. These self-styling drapery tapes can also be used for valances and attached to a flat tension rod with standard drapery hooks.

A valance is a special finishing touch on a shower curtain. It helps to enclose the space and coordinate the room. Most of the valance top treatments used for windows are appropriate shower curtain headings as well. The cloud, pouf, and smocked valances are soft, light treatments; the straight lines of pleated and flat valances are more tailored.

Trim a shower curtain with lace, eyelet, ruffling, or grosgrain or satin ribbon.

✂ Cutting Directions

Cut two 81" (206 cm) lengths of fabric (extra fabric will be needed for matching prints); stitch lengths together. Cut shower curtain 6" (15 cm) wider and 9" (23 cm) longer than vinyl liner.

Cut valance width 2½ times the length of rod, and the desired length plus 6½" (16.3 cm) for heading and hems. Seam together as necessary for desired width. Cut smocking tape the cut width of the valance, plus a little extra for aligning and finishing ends.

YOU WILL NEED

Shower curtain fabric, 4½ yd. (4.15 m) for standard liner; extra needed for matching prints.

Drapery folding tape, 2⅛ yd. (1.95 m) for shower curtain; smocking tape for valance, 2½ times the length of the rod.

Vinyl shower curtain liner, 70" × 72" (178 × 183 cm); 12 metal shower curtain rings; flat tension rod for valance.

Drapery hooks.

How to Sew a Shower Curtain

1) Turn under and stitch double 1" (2.5 cm) side hems. At bottom edge, make a double 3" (7.5 cm) hem. At top, press under 1" (2.5 cm). Do not stitch.

2) Remove pull-cords from folding tape. You will use hook loops only. With loop side facing you and toward the top, pin tape on wrong side of fabric ½" (1.3 cm) from upper edge. Turn under raw edge at ends of tape; stitch in place.

3) Insert shower curtain rings into holes of vinyl liner and into hook loops of folding tape. Hang on shower curtain rod.

How to Sew a Smocked Shower Curtain Valance

1) Stitch double 1" (2.5 cm) side hems; stitch double 2" (5 cm) bottom hem; turn upper edge under 2½" (6.5 cm), and press.

2) Pin smocking tape ½" (1.3 cm) from upper folded edge with loops on top. Turn under 1" (2.5 cm) of tape at each end, and lift out strings. Stitch both sides of tape.

3) Knot strings securely to prevent them from being pulled out. Pull up strings to smock, adjusting fullness to fit rod. Insert drapery hooks every 3" to 4" (7.5 to 10 cm). Mount flat tension rod; hang valance from rod.

Shower Curtain Ideas

Pouf valance. Make valance (page 60). Mount valance on tension rods. The valance may be mounted at ceiling or just above shower curtain rod.

Eyelet-trimmed curtain. Stitch flat eyelet to curtain in ½" (1.3 cm) seam. Press. Turn under seam allowance; stitch narrow hem.

Box-pleated valance. Use plaid or stripe as guide to make box-pleated valance. Attach separate rod pocket, and cover stitching line with satin or grosgrain ribbon. Mount valance on tension rod.

Cloud valance. Make a rod-pocket valance. Pull up hem into evenly spaced poufs; hand-tack. Mount curtain panels and valance on tension rods, with plastic liner on installed shower curtain rod.

Cushions
& Pillows

Boxed Cushions with Welting

To update any room in the house, make new covers for loose cushions on chairs, benches, or window seats. Boxed cushions may be firm or soft, depending on the foam used. Foam is available in several thicknesses and densities. Use firm or medium density foam for seat cushions; select soft density foam for back cushions. Wrap the foam with bonded polyester batting to keep the cover from shifting and to soften the look of boxed cushions.

Install a zipper across the back of the cover, extending around about 4" (10 cm) on each of the two sides to make it easier to insert the cushion into the finished cover. Or install a zipper across only the back side for cushions that will be exposed on three sides. Use an upholstery zipper, available in lengths longer than dressmaker zippers. The tab of the zipper will be hidden in a pocket at the end of the zipper opening. The concealed tab is an upholstery touch that gives a professional finish to the cushion.

✂ Cutting Directions

Cut top and bottom pieces 1" (2.5 cm) larger than finished cushion size to allow for seam allowances. Cut foam same size as top and bottom pieces for a firm, tight fit. Cut two zipper strips, each the length of the zipper tape; each zipper strip is half the thickness of finished cushion plus 1" (2.5 cm) for seam allowances. Cut boxing strip the length of cushion front plus twice the length of cushion side. Cut welting strips 1½" (3.8 cm) wide, with length 2 times the circumference of the cushion plus seam allowances.

YOU WILL NEED

Decorator fabric for top, bottom, boxing strips, and welting.

Upholstery bonded polyester batting to wrap all sides of cushion.

Foam in desired density and thickness.

Upholstery zipper, about 8" (20.5 cm) longer than back width measurement of cushion.

5/32" (3.8 mm) cording, slightly more than 2 times the circumference of the cushion.

How to Make a Boxed Cushion

1) Measure width and depth of cushion area to determine the size of finished cushion. Determine thickness of foam.

2) Cut fabric and foam. Mark the wrong side of fabric pieces with chalk.

3) Press under ½" (1.3 cm) seam allowance on one long edge of each zipper strip. Position folded edges of strips along center of zipper teeth. Using zipper foot, topstitch ⅜" (1 cm) from folds.

4) Press under 2" (5 cm) on one short end of boxing strip. Lap the boxing strip over the zipper strip to cover zipper tab. Stitch through all layers 1½" (3.8 cm) from folded edge of boxing strip. If desired, edgestitch along fold to within 1" (2.5 cm) of centered zipper.

5) Cover cording, page 29, step 1. Using zipper foot, stitch welting to right side of top and bottom pieces. Stop 1" (2.5 cm) from corner; make diagonal clip to stitching.

(Continued on next page)

6) Make additional clips as necessary to allow welting to ease around corners. Join ends of welting as in steps 3 to 5, page 29.

7) Place boxing strip on cushion top, right sides together; center zipper on back edge. Start stitching 2" (5 cm) from end of boxing strip, crowding welt. Clip corners as approached; stop stitching 4" (10 cm) before starting point.

8) Clip to mark seam allowances at ends of boxing strip. Stitch boxing strip ends together. Trim excess fabric; finger press seam open. Finish stitching boxing strip to cushion top.

9) Fold boxing strip, and clip seam allowance to mark bottom corners; be sure all four corners are lined up with cushion top corners. Open zipper.

10) Place boxing strip and cushion bottom, right sides together. Match clips of boxing strip to bottom corners. Stitch. Turn cover right side out.

11) Wrap cushion with batting; whipstitch in place. Fold cushion to insert in cover. Wrap with plastic to help slide cushion into cover if necessary. Remove plastic.

12) Smooth batting; stretch cover from front to back. Close zipper. Smooth cushion from center to edges. Stretch welting taut from corner to corner to square cushion.

How to Match Patterns on a Boxed Cushion

Alternative zipper placement. Install zipper across the back of the cushion, without extending it around the sides, if cushion will be exposed on three sides. The boxing strip may require piecing.

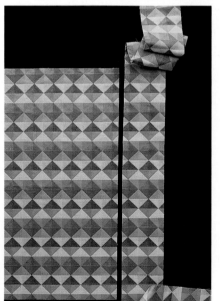

1) Cut cushion top, boxing strip, and bottom to match pattern at front seamlines. For reversible cushion, match pattern from cushion top, down boxing strip, and continue to the back.

2) Notch corners of boxing strip. Join boxing strip to cushion top and bottom, stitching front edge first. Then stitch along other sides of cushion.

Button-tufted Cushions

Add seating comfort to wooden chairs and benches with simple knife-edge, button-tufted cushions. The lightly padded inner cushion is created by covering a piece of foam with a layer of polyester upholstery batting. The button tufting prevents the cushion from shifting inside the cover and also adds detailing. Place one button on the top and one on the bottom of the cushion, and pull them tight with strands of thread to create an indentation. Welting can be inserted into the seam for additional interest.

You may want to make the covered buttons and welting from a fabric that contrasts with that of the seat cushion. Checked and striped fabrics can create interesting effects when used for welting.

Secure the seat cushion to the chairs or bench ties, if necessary. Place a set of ties near each back corner of the cushion for securing it to the back posts of the chair or bench.

✂ Cutting Directions

Make the pattern and cut the fabric, foam, and batting following steps 1 to 3, on page 114. For the optional welting, cut 1⅝" (4 cm) bias fabric strips; piece the strips as necessary to make a length that is equal to the circumference of the cushion plus at least 1" (2.5 cm) overlap at the ends. For each tie, cut two 1½" (3.8 cm) fabric strips 10" to 16" (25.5 to 40.5 cm) long.

YOU WILL NEED

Decorator fabric.

Contrasting decorator fabric, for buttons and welting, optional.

Polyurethane foam, 1" (2.5 cm) thick.

Polyester upholstery batting; polyester fiberfill, optional.

Cording, 5/32" (3.8 mm) in diameter, for welting, optional.

Upholstery buttons or flat dressmaker buttons with strong shank; two for each button placement.

Buttonhole twist or carpet thread; long needle with large eye.

How to Sew a Button-tufted Cushion

1) Make a paper pattern of seat to be covered by cushion, rounding any sharp corners; simplify shape as necessary. Cut pattern; check the fit. Mark pattern for placement of ties, if desired.

2) Cut two pieces of polyester upholstery batting, using pattern. Position pattern on foam; trace, using marking pen. Cut foam ¼" (6 mm) inside marked line, using electric or serrated knife.

3) Position the pattern on wrong side of decorator fabric. Mark cutting line 1" (2.5 cm) from edge of pattern; this allows ½" (1.3 cm) for the seam allowances and ½" (1.3 cm) for the thickness of the foam and batting. Cut the cushion top on marked line. Cut cushion bottom, using cushion top as pattern.

4) Make welting, if desired, and apply to cushion top as on page 29, steps 1 to 5. Make ties, if desired, as on page 118, step 3. Pin ties to the right side of seat top at markings, with raw edges even; stitch in place.

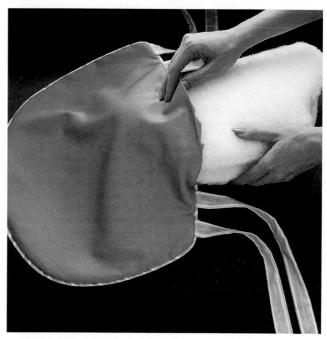

5) Position cushion top and bottom with right sides together and raw edges even. Stitch ½" (1.3 cm) seam; leave center opening along back edge for inserting cushion. Trim the seam allowances and clip curves. If welting is not used, press seam open. Turn right side out; lightly press.

6) Prepare and insert cushion as in step 11, page 111. Slipstitch opening closed.

7) Pin-mark button placement on both sides of cushion as desired. Cut two or three 18" (46 cm) strands of buttonhole twist or carpet thread; insert all strands through button shank, and secure at middle of thread length with a double knot.

8) Insert the ends of the thread strands through the eye of a long needle. Insert needle through cushion to back side. Remove strands from needle; divide strands into two groups.

9) Thread second button on one thread group; tie a single knot, using both thread groups; pull until buttons are tight against cushion, creating indentation. Wrap the thread two or three times around the button shank. Tie a double knot; trim thread tails.

Tie-tab Pillows

Tie-tab pillows are created by covering a knife-edge inner pillow with a pillowcase that has a tie-tab closure on one side. The tabs on the case can be tied in knots or bows, depending on the look desired. This pillow style provides an opportunity to combine coordinating fabrics, because the inner pillow is visible between the tie tabs along the closure side.

The number of tabs needed will vary with the size of the pillow. Two tabs are needed for each tie. Evenly space the tabs about 3" to 4" (7.5 to 10 cm) apart.

The instructions that follow are for a knife-edge inner pillow and a tie-tab pillowcase with tapered corners. Tapering the stitching at the corners eliminates dog-eared corners on the finished pillow. If you are making the inner pillow or the pillowcase from a plaid or striped fabric, you may prefer not to taper the corners.

✂ Cutting Directions

For the knife-edge inner pillow, cut the pillow front and back 1" (2.5 cm) wider and longer than the pillow form.

For the pillowcase, cut the case front and back ½" (1.3 cm) wider and 1" (2.5 cm) longer than the pillow form. Also cut a facing strip 1½" (3.8 cm) wide, with the length equal to two times the length of the pillow form plus 1" (2.5 cm). For each tab, cut two 1¼" (3.2 cm) strips of fabric. For knotted tabs, cut the strips 8" (20.5 cm) long; for tabs tied into bows, cut the strips 12" (30.5 cm) long.

YOU WILL NEED

Decorator fabric, for inner pillow, pillowcase, and tabs.

Pillow form.

How to Sew a Knife-edge Pillow

1) Fold pillow front into fourths. For tapered corners, mark a point halfway between corner and fold on each open side. At corner, mark a point ⅜" (1 cm) from each raw edge. Mark lines, tapering from the raw edges at center marks to marks at corner. Cut along the marked lines.

2) Use pillow front as a pattern for cutting pillow back. Pin the pillow front to pillow back, right sides together. Stitch a ½" (1.3 cm) seam, leaving opening on one side for turning and for inserting pillow form.

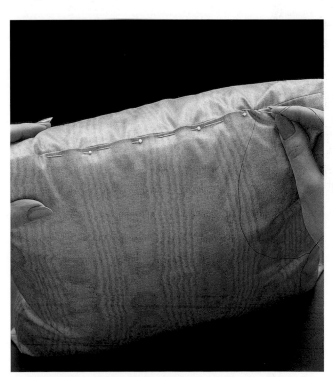

3) Turn pillow cover right side out. Press under seam allowances at opening. Insert pillow form. Pin opening closed; slipstitch or edgestitch close to folded edge.

How to Sew a Tie-tab Pillowcase

1) Fold pillowcase front in half. Mark and cut tapered corners at one end as on page 117, steps 1 and 2; do not taper corners at edge of case where the ties will be stitched. Use case front as a pattern for case back.

2) Pin case front to case back, right sides together. Stitch around sides, using a ½" (1.3 cm) seam allowance and leaving untapered edge unstitched; press seams open. Turn the case right side out, pulling out the corners.

3) Place two tab strips right sides together, matching the raw edges. Stitch ¼" (6 mm) seam around long sides and one end of tab. Repeat for remaining tabs. Trim corners, and turn the tabs right side out; press.

4) Pin tabs to right side of the case along unstitched edge, keeping the raw edges even and spacing the tabs evenly; position end tabs about 2½" (6.5 cm) from the seam.

5) Fold facing strip, right sides together, matching short ends; stitch ½" (1.3 cm) seam. Press the seam open. Press up ¼" (6 mm) along one edge of the facing strip.

6) Pin unpressed edge of facing strip to open edge of pillowcase, right sides together and raw edges even. Stitch ½" (1.3 cm) seam; trim the seam allowance. Press facing to the wrong side of the case.

7) Machine-stitch or hand-stitch facing in place. Insert pillow. Tie tabs into bows or knots.

Mock Box Pillows

Mock box pillows are easy to make, with pleated corners that are simply folded in place. Suitable for any decorating style, the pillows may be plain or trimmed with welting. Large pillows can be stacked for use as floor pillows, or smaller ones used as accent pillows.

Pleated corners and a welted "waistline" accent the overstuffed look of these mock box pillows. They can be made in sizes suitable for throw pillows or for floor cushions. Pillow forms are available in many sizes, up to 30" (76 cm) square. Follow the chart below to determine the pillow form size and cutting dimensions of the pillow front and back.

YOU WILL NEED

Fabric for pillow front and back.
Contrasting fabric and cording, for welting.
Pillow form in size indicated in chart.

✂ Cutting Directions

Finished Length × Width	Finished Depth	Form Size	Cut Length × Width
22" × 22" (56 × 56 cm)	8" (20.5 cm)	30" (76 cm)	31" × 31" (78.5 × 78.5 cm)
18" × 18" (46 × 46 cm)	6" (15 cm)	24" (61 cm)	25" × 25" (63.5 × 63.5 cm)
16" × 16" (40.5 × 40.5 cm)	4" (10 cm)	20" (51 cm)	21" × 21" (53.5 × 53.5 cm)

How to Sew a Mock Box Pillow

1) Mark a square on right side of pillow front at one corner, with each side measuring one-half the desired finished depth plus ½" (1.3 cm). Draw diagonal line through square.

2) Fold fabric on marked lines of square, bringing fold to diagonal line; pin. Baste across pleats within ½" (1.3 cm) seam allowance. Trim off triangular section of excess fabric.

3) Repeat steps 1 and 2 for each corner of front and back. Attach welting to pillow front as in steps 1 to 5, page 29. Pin pillow front to back, right sides together, matching corner pleats. Stitch, crowding welting; leave an opening for turning.

4) Turn pillow right side out through opening. Punch in pillow form corners; insert into pillow. Slipstitch opening closed.

Double-flange Pillows

Double-flange pillows have an understated look and exceptional versatility. Made from brocades and tapestries, they are elegant in a traditional setting, yet their streamlined design makes them equally elegant in contemporary prints and solids. Select floral prints of polished cotton, and these pillows are right at home in a country room. For these pillows, two mitered panels are stitched together along the inner edge of the border, creating a double flange. At the center of the pillow, a matching or contrasting fabric is tucked under the flange before the pillow front and back are joined.

✂ Cutting Directions

The size of the inner portion of the pillow is equal to the size of the pillow form. To this measurement, add four times the desired width of the flange plus ½" (1.3 cm) for turning under the raw edges; cut two pieces of fabric this size, for the pillow front and back. For example, for a 14" (35.5 cm) square pillow with a 2½" (6.5 cm) flange, use a 14" (35.5 cm) pillow form, and cut two pieces, each 24½" (62.3 cm) square. For the center insert, add twice the desired depth of the flange to the size of the pillow form; cut one piece of insert fabric.

YOU WILL NEED

Fabric for pillow front and pillow back, including flange, yardage depending on size of project; for 14" (35.5 cm) pillow form and 2½" (6.5 cm) flange, you will need ¾ yd. (0.7 m) of 54" (137 cm) fabric.

Fabric for insert at center of pillow; yardage depending on size of project; for 14" (35.5 cm) pillow form, you will need ⅝ yd. (0.6 m).

Pillow form in desired size.

Polyester fiberfill, for filling out corners.

How to Sew a Double-flange Pillow with an Insert

1) Stitch scant ¼" (6 mm) from edges of pillow front. Fold edges to the wrong side; press just beyond the stitching line. On each side, press under desired depth of flange.

2) Open out the corner; fold diagonally so pressed folds match (arrows). Press diagonal fold.

3) Open out the corner. Fold through center of corner, right sides together. Stitch on diagonal fold-line from step 2. Trim fabric at corner ¼" (6 mm) from stitching. Press seam open.

4) Press the flange in place, turning the corners right side out. Place insert fabric on pillow front, tucking raw edges under flange; smooth, and pin in place.

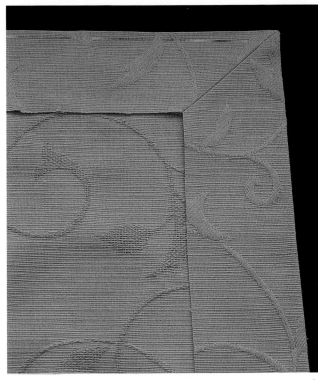

5) Press under sides of pillow back, an amount equal to depth of flange plus ¼" (6 mm), so fabric on folded flange is right side up. Miter corners as in steps 2 to 4.

6) Place pillow front on pillow back, with mitered sides up, matching edges; pin.

7) Stitch around inner edge of flange, securing the insert; pivot at corners, and leave opening on one side for inserting pillow form.

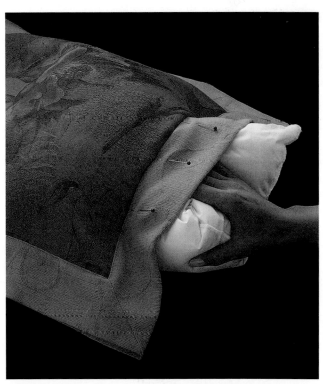

8) Insert the pillow form; push fiberfill into the corners of the pillow as necessary to fill out pillow. Pin the opening closed; complete stitching on inner edge of flange.

Index

A

Acetate, 15
Accents, decorative, 24-29, 100-101
Adhesive-backed hook and loop tape, 99
Antique satin, 15
Atmosphere, creating, 12-13
Austrian valance, 62-63

B

Band trims, 25
Bathrooms,
  decorating plans for, 10
  sewing for, 76, 98-105
Batting,
  boxed cushion, 108-111
  padded cornices, 71-73
Bed skirts,
  see Dust skirt
Bedcovers
  duvet covers, 78-81, 86-87
  futon covers, 91-93
  measuring for, 76-77
  reverse sham, 88-89
Bedrooms,
  decorating plans for, 10
  sewing for, 76-97
Beds,
  dust skirts, 82-83
  duvet covers, 78-81, 86-87
  futon covers, 91-93
  measuring, 76
  reverse sham bedcover, 88-89
Bedspread,
  see Bedcovers
Bias strips, 28, 88
Bishop sleeve curtains, 55
Borders, 84-85
Box pillows, mock, 120-121
Boxed cushions, 108-111
Box-pleated valance, 104
Braid, 25
Braided tiebacks, 43
Buckram, 15, 36-41, 45
Button-tufted cushions, 113-115

C

Cascades, 59, 66
Casement fabrics, 14
Casings,
  see Rod pockets
Chintz, 15, 51
Cloud valance, 105
Color schemes
  planning for, 10
  selection, 13, 16
Comforters,
  see Duvet covers
Conventional traverse rods, 35
  pinch-pleated draperies, 36
Cording,
  also see Welting
  boxed cushions with welting, 108-111
  encasing, 43
  jumbo sizes, 42, 44
  shirred insert tieback, 45
  sizes for welting, 28
  tuck-pleated dust skirt and shams, 82-85
  twisted, 25
Corners,
  on boxed cushions, 109-111
  mitered, 25, 27, 84-85
  outside edge corners, 27
  rounding corners, 29
  squaring sheet corners, 77
Cornices, 59
  building, 71
  padded, 71-73
  reverse roll-up shade, 52-53
Cotton 14-16
Covers,
  see Bedcovers
Curtain hardware, 34-35
Curtain lengths and widths, 32-33
Curtain rods, 34-35
Curtains,
  bishop sleeve, 55
  hourglass, 46-50
  matching prints, 20-21
  measuring for, 32-33
  shower, 102-105
  tent-flap, 56-57
  tiebacks for, 42-45
Cushions,
  boxed, 108-111
  button-tufted, 113-115
  cleaning, 17
Cutting,
  also see specific items to sew
  matching prints, 20
  sheets, 77
  welting strips, 29

D

Decorating, guidelines for, 13
Decorative traverse rods, 34
  pinch-pleated draperies, 36
Decorator fabric, 15-17
  also see Fabric

Designer,
  as a source of ideas, 10
  tips from, 18
Differential feed, for ruffles, 26
Double pouf valance, 59, 61
Double-flange pillows, 123-125
Double-fold hems, 22-23, 41
Dowels, wooden,
  Austrian valance, 62-63
  fabric screen, 94-95
  reverse roll-up shade, 52-53
Draperies,
  care, 17
  dressing, 41
  hardware, 34-35
  length fluctuations, 17
  lining for, 17, 40-41
  measuring for, 32-33
  pinch-pleated, 36-41
  pleat worksheet, 37
  stackback, 36, 59
  tiebacks for, 42-45
Drapery hooks, 39
Dressing draperies, 41
Drycleaning fabrics, 17
Duck fabric, 16
Dust skirt, tuck-pleated, 82-83
Duvet covers, 78-81, 86-87
  with ruffle and welting, 81
  ruffled, 80-81
  sheet requirements for, 77
  from sheets, 86-87
  with welting, 79
Dye lots, 16

E

Edgings, 25
Embellished towels, 100-101
Encasing cording, 43
Ends, squaring, 20-21
Estimating yardage, 32, 37
  also see Measuring
Eyelet,
  see Lace

F

Fabric,
  also see specific items to sew
  care, 17
  cost considerations, 14
  crease-resistant finish, 15
  decorator fabric, 15-17
  decorator vs. garment, 15
  dye lots, 16
  estimating yardage, 32, 37
  fiber content, 15
  mixing patterns, 18
  preshrinking, 15
  protective finishes, 17
  railroading, 21, 71
  rosettes, 51
  selection, 14-15

thread count, 14
top treatments, 59
upholstery, 16
weave, 14
welting strips, 28
Fabric screen, 94-95
Fiber content, 15
Filling,
  see Batting
Finger pressing draperies, 39
French seams, 22
Fringe, 25
  Austrian valance, 62-63
Fullness, estimated yardage for, 32-33
Futon covers, 91-93

G

Garment fabric, 15
Gathered sink and vanity skirts, 98-99
Gimp, 25
Guidelines for decorating, 13

H

Hardware, curtain and drapery, 34-35
Headings,
  also see specific items to sew
  measuring for 32-33
  ruffles with, 27
Hems, 22-23
  measuring for, 32-33
Holdbacks, 35
Hook and loop tape, 82-83, 98-99
Hourglass curtains, 46-50

J

Jabots, 59, 66-69
Jumbo welted tiebacks, 42-44

K

Kitchen-family room area, decorating
  plans for, 10
Knife-edge pillow, 117

L

Lace, 14
  edgings, 25
  embellished towels, 100-101
  estimating fullness, 32-33
Laundering fabric, 17
Length, drapery,
  determining, 32-33
  fluctuations, 17

Linen, 14-15
Lining,
  see specific items to sew
Living-dining area, decorating plans
  for, 10
Loop fringe, 25

M

Master bedroom, decorating plans
  for, 10
Matching patterns, boxed
  cushions, 111
Matching prints, 20-21
Measuring,
  also see specific items to sew
  bed dimensions, 76
  top treatments, 59
  windows, 32-33
Mitering,
  outside edges, 27
  trimming, 25
  tuck-pleated pillow sham, 84-85
Mock box pillows, 120-121
Monograms, 101
Mounting,
  see specific items
Mounting board, 66, 69
Muslin, swags and jabots, 66

N

Nylon velvets, 16

O

Overlock hems, 22
Overlock seams, 22-23

P

Padded cornices, 71-73
Pattern repeats on window
  treatments, 33
Patterns,
  fabric requirements for matching,
   32-33
  matching on a boxed cushion, 111
  measuring for, 32-33
  mixing, 18
Pillow shams,
  reverse sham bedcover, 88-89
  tuck-pleated, 84-85
Pillows,
  double-flange, 123-125
  knife-edge, 117
  mock box, 120-121
  tie-tab, 116-119

Pinch-pleated draperies, 36-41
  estimating yardage, 37
  lined, 40-41
  pleat worksheet, 37
  unlined, 38-39
Piping,
  see Cording, Welting
Plain seams, 22
Planning techniques, 10
Pleats,
  box-pleated valance, 104
  pinch, 36-41
  tuck-pleated dust skirt and shams,
   82-85
Polyester, 14-15
Pouf valance, 59-61
  shower curtains, 104
Preshrinking fabric, 15, 100
Prints,
  combination, 18
  matching, 20-21
  miniprints, 18
Protective finishes, 17

R

Railroading,
  padded cornices, 71
  wide fabrics, 21
Rayon, 15
Record keeping, 10
Repeat, pattern, 33
Reverse roll-up shade, 52-53
Reverse sham bedcover, 88-89
Ribbons,
  embellished towels, 100-101
  trimming with, 25
Rings, curtain, 34, 43-45
Rod pockets,
  also see specific items to sew
  measuring for, 32-33
Rolled edge, 22
Rosettes, fabric, 51
Ruffled duvet cover, 80-81
Ruffled tapered valance, 64-65
Ruffler attachment, 26, 80
Ruffles,
  gathering, 26-27
  heading for, 27

S

Sailcloth, 16
Sash rods, 35
Satin edge, 22
Saucer as pattern guide,
  reverse sham bedcover, 88
  tuck-pleated dust skirt, 82
Scallop treatments,
  hiding seams, 22
  valances, 59
Screens, fabric, 94-95

Seams, 22-23
  measuring for, 33
Self-ruffle, duvet covers, 78, 80-81
Serged hems, 22
Serged seams, 22-23
Sewing with a plan, 10
Shade, reverse roll-up, 52-53
Sham bedcover, reverse, 88-89
Shams, pillow,
  see Pillow shams
Sheer fabric, 14
  railroading, 21
Sheets, 77
  for dust skirt deck, 82-83
  for duvet covers, 77, 86-87
  squaring corners for, 77
  for test swags, 66
Shirred insert tieback, 45
Shirred jumbo welting tieback, 44
Shirring foot,
  for ruffled duvet cover, 80
  for ruffles, 26
Shower curtains, 102-105
Side hems, 22
Sink, skirt for, 98-99
Smocked shower curtain valance, 103
Squaring corners,
  also see Mitering
  of sheets, 77
Squaring fabric ends, 20
Stackback, 59
  pinch-pleated draperies, 36
Straightening crosswise ends, 21
Stripes, 18
Swagged table topper, 97
Swags, 59, 66-69
  attaching to mounting board, 66, 69
  estimating size, 66
  holders, 35

T

Table topper, swagged, 97
Tapered valance, 64-65
Tasseled fringe, 25
Tasseled tiebacks, 25
Tension rods, 35
Tent-flap curtains, 56-57
Texture, as design consideration, 13
Thread count, 14
  in garment fabric, 15
Tie-tab pillows, 116-119
Tiebacks, 42-45
  bishop sleeve curtains, 55
  braided, 43
  cord-and-tassel, 35
  encasing cording, 43
  holders, 35
  jumbo knotted, 44
  jumbo twist, 44
  jumbo welting, 42
  shirred insert, 45
  shirred jumbo welting, 44
  tasseled, 25
Tissue paper, for poufs, 55

Top treatments, 59-73
  measuring for, 59
Towels, embellished, 100-101
Traverse rods,
  conventional, 35
  decorative, 34
  flexible, 35
Trimming, accent with, 24-29, 100-101
Tuck-pleated dust skirt, 82-83
Tuck-pleated pillow sham, 84-85
Twisted cords, 25

U

Underdraperies, 32
  clearance for top treatments, 59
Upholstery fabric, 16
Upholstery zipper, 108
Utility rod, 35, 52-53

V

Valances, 59
  Austrian, 62-63
  box-pleated, 104
  cloud, 105
  double pouf, 59, 61
  pouf, 59-60, 104
  shower curtain, 102-105
  tapered, 64-65
Vanity skirt, 98-99

W

Warp sateen, 15
Weave, fabric, 14
  drapery length and, 17
Welting,
  boxed cushions, 108-111
  cord sizes, 28
  decorative, 28-29
  duvet covers, 78-81
  encasing cording, 43
  making and attaching, 29
  padded cornices, 71-73
  tiebacks, 42-45
  tuck-pleated dust skirt and sham,
    82-85
Wide fabrics, railroading, 21
Width, drapery, 32-33
Window measurement, 32-33
Window treatments, 31-73
  also see Cornices, Curtains,
    Draperies, Shades, Tiebacks,
    Top treatments, Valances
  bishop sleeve curtains, 55
  curtain and drapery hardware, 34-35
  dressing draperies, 41
  hourglass curtains, 46-50
  matching prints, 20-21
  measuring windows, 32-33

pinch-pleated draperies, 36-41
reverse roll-up shades, 52-53
seams and hems, 22-23
tent-flap curtains, 56-57
tiebacks, 42-45
top treatments, 59-73
Wood poles, 34
  drapery hooks, 39
Wooden dowels,
  see Dowels

Y

Yardage estimating charts, 32, 37

Z

Zigzag stitch, for ruffles, 26
Zippers,
  boxed cushions, 108-111
  duvet covers 78-81, 86-87
  tuck-pleated pillow sham, 84-85
  upholstery, 108